INSTITUTE OF LEADERSHIP & MANAGEMENT **ilm**

SUPERSERIES

Controlling Costs

FOURTH EDITION

Published for the
Institute of Leadership & Management by

Pergamon
Flexible
Learning

OXFORD   AMSTERDAM   BOSTON   LONDON   NEW YORK   PARIS
SAN DIEGO   SAN FRANCISCO   SINGAPORE   SYDNEY   TOKYO

Pergamon Flexible Learning
An imprint of Elsevier Science
Linacre House, Jordan Hill, Oxford OX2 8DP
200 Wheeler Road, Burlington, MA 01803

First published 1986
Second edition 1991
Third edition 1997
Fourth edition 2003

British Library Cataloguing in Publication Data
A catalogue record for this book is available from the British Library

ISBN 0 7506 5842 8

For information on Pergamon Flexible Learning
visit our website at www.bh.com/pergamonfl

Institute of Leadership & Management
registered office
1 Giltspur Street
London
EC1A 9DD
Telephone 020 7294 3053
www.i-l-m.com
ILM is a subsidiary of the City & Guilds Group

The views expressed in this work are those of the authors and do
not necessarily reflect those of the Institute of Leadership &
Management or of the publisher

Authors: Raymond Taylor and Clare Donnelly
Editor: Clare Donnelly
Editorial management: Genesys, www.genesys-consultants.com
Based on previous material by: Peter Elliot
Composition by Genesis Typesetting, Rochester, Kent
Printed and bound in Great Britain by MPG Books, Bodmin

Contents

Contents

Workbook introduction

1 ILM Super Series study links

This workbook addresses the issues of *Controlling Costs*. Should you wish to extend your study to other Super Series workbooks covering related or different subject areas, you will find a comprehensive list at the back of this book.

2 Links to ILM Qualifications

This workbook relates to the following learning outcomes in segments from the ILM Level 3 Introductory Certificate in First Line Management and the Level 3 Certificate in First Line Management.

C6.2   Working to a budget
3   Recognise ways of reducing or eliminating unacceptable variances
4   Contribute to the formulation of budgets by providing relevant data and/or making appropriate recommendations.

C6.3   Understanding costs
1   Identify the elements of costs, their behaviour and the need for their control
2   Appreciate the value of standard costing and its role as a control mechanism
3   Identify, recommend and implement measures to control and/or reduce costs.

3 Links to S/NVQs in Management

This workbook relates to the following elements of the Management Standards which are used in S/NVQs in Management, as well as a range of other S/NVQs.

B1.1   Make recommendations for the use of resources
B1.2   Contribute to the control of resources.

It will also help you to develop the following Personal Competences:

- focus on results
- thinking and taking decisions.

4 Workbook objectives

In our daily lives we all need to control expenditure (another name for costs), so that we have money to spend and save. Companies also need to control costs to help them make a profit and reinvest for the future. Business organizations must be competitive to survive, so keeping costs under control is an essential activity. Other organizations need to control costs to make the best use of resources.

We need to distinguish between cost control and cost reduction. Cost reduction is usually undertaken as a systematic programme to reduce existing levels of costs, perhaps because a company is facing difficulties, or needs to be able to match the prices of competitors. It may involve changing working methods, new sources of supply, or employing fewer people.

Cost control is a continuous and routine management function. It is almost certainly part of your job, for costs aren't just the concern of accountants and senior managers. What's more, you and your workteam contribute to the final cost of whatever goods or services you provide, so it is important that you take an active interest in cost control.

In this workbook we will look at ways of controlling and monitoring costs. You will improve your understanding of these matters so that you and your workteam can be more effective.

Throughout the workbook we look at examples from different organizations. Some may or may not be directly relevant to you at the moment, but the principles may be appropriate to something you do at work. Costing techniques were developed for practical purposes. You should use them when relevant and not when they would be too costly to use or of little benefit. Of course, this means that you must be aware of what is available to you. Remember that there is value in a breadth of knowledge, even where something does not immediately appear relevant to you.

4.1 Objectives

When you have completed this workbook you will be better able to:

- identify different costs and how they behave;
- appreciate how important it is to control costs;
- understand how standard costing techniques help to control costs;
- use different methods for controlling and reducing costs;
- help to draw up workable budgets.

5 Activity planner

The following Activities need some planning and you may want to look at them now.

Activity 10   Here you are being asked to think about obtaining 'value for money' from your workteam and you may like to think about this as you study your workbook before reaching that activity.

Activity 13   Here you are being asked to think about breakdowns in production or delivery of service and ways in which you could counteract these problems.

Activity 34   You are invited to consider how to communicate the need for cost consciousness to your workteam.

Some or all of these Activities may provide the basis of evidence for your S/NVQ portfolio. All Portfolio Activities and the Work-based assignment (on page 90) are sign-posted with this icon:

This icon will always show the elements to which the activity or Work-based assignment relates.

Note that the Work-based assignment suggests that you speak to your manager, finance director or to your colleagues in the accounts office about the way in which costs are controlled in your organization.

You might like to start thinking now about who to approach and arrange to speak with them.

Session A
Classifying costs

1 Introduction

At home, if your expenses or costs are high in comparison to your income, your life can be difficult. Say, for example, that the electricity, gas and telephone bills are all due at the same time and your wages are only enough to pay two of them. What do you do?

Let's assume you negotiate time to pay but realize that the same problem is likely to occur next quarter. You'll have to decide whether to turn down the heating, switch off the lights or cut back on phone calls.

Businesses can find themselves in similar situations. It is up to you and everyone in your organization to be concerned about the costs of whatever you produce or supply, just as you should be concerned about quality.

Business organizations in the private sector who do not control costs may go out of business. Organizations in the public sector with high and increasing costs will need to make severe cuts in their activities and will attract a great deal of criticism from the public and government of the day. As a first line manager, you'll need to be concerned with costs and their control.

In this session we will look at the different kinds of cost and how you can help to control them.

2 Organizational costs

The **total costs** of an organization are made up of such things as:

- wages and salaries;
- electricity, gas and other utilities;
- purchase of steel, wood, stationery, X-ray plates or whatever raw materials the organization uses;
- payments for services from transport to cleaning.

These costs are deducted from the **sales** of the organization; the difference is **profit**. Profit might also be called operating surplus by organizations in the public and voluntary sectors.

Sales (or income) – Costs = Profit (or operating surplus)

> Several ways of setting prices are based on the idea of determining costs and then adding a percentage for profit. Identifying costs is, therefore, important.

The implication of this is that an organization can either **increase its prices** or **decrease its costs** to become more profitable or to alter the level of its operating surplus.

But, there are dangers with these courses of action.

Activity 1

3 mins

Suppose the price of your favourite biscuits was suddenly doubled.

Jot down **three** things you might do.

_____

_____

_____

_____

EXTENSION 1
You can explore the relationship of costs and pricing further in Kirkland's and Howard's book, *Simple and Practical Costing, Pricing and Credit Control.*

You might:

■ buy fewer biscuits;
■ stop buying the biscuits;
■ buy biscuits made by a competitor;
■ buy an alternative product, such as cake;
■ cut back on something else so you could afford the biscuits.

People who buy your organization's products may choose one of these options if you increase your prices. You probably don't have much to do with fixing selling prices, but you **are** in a position to affect costs. By controlling these you can help your organization, and that's what we'll concentrate on.

As a first line manager you will be concerned with the following costs:

■ labour costs;
■ materials costs;
■ overheads.

3 Labour costs

The total 'labour cost' of employing people in the organization comprises the wages or salaries that they receive directly, plus the additional costs to the employer of National Insurance contributions, pension contributions and other benefits. It depends on the type of organization, but the costs of labour are often the most significant cost of all.

If the organization makes something that is sold or supplied, then its total labour cost is often split into direct and indirect labour costs.

Wages that can be identified with a particular product are usually called **direct labour costs**. Some examples of direct labour are:

■ painting a product;
■ welding a part;
■ sewing a garment;
■ dealing with customers;
■ processing data;
■ a hairdresser doing a cut and blow dry.

Wages that cannot be identified with a particular product are **indirect labour costs**. Examples of indirect labour can arise from a number of activities, such as:

- maintenance costs;
- cleaning;
- employing a sales force;
- operating a marketing department.

None of these can be identified directly with a particular item of production, even though they are essential for an organization as a whole.

Direct labour costs will increase or decrease in proportion to the production activity being carried out and for this reason are called **variable costs**.

Indirect labour costs happen all the time, whether something is being produced or not. They are **fixed costs**.

We will look at the significance of fixed and variable costs a little later on.

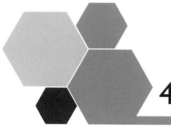

4 Materials costs

In manufacturing, materials costs can often account for more than half of the total costs of production.

In industries such as aero engineering and computer manufacturing, you can appreciate that the costs of materials such as steel, plastic and microchips will probably make up much of the total costs of the finished product. Conversely, a telephone banking operation or call centre may find that materials costs account for much less than one tenth of total costs.

We already know that labour costs can be broken down into direct and indirect categories. Materials costs can also be divided into:

- direct materials costs;
- indirect materials costs.

Direct materials costs are the costs of materials used in the products, such as:

- wood;
- steel;
- paper;

- component parts;
- ingredients for meals;
- plant food and compost.

Direct materials costs can be identified directly and in total with an item being produced.

Indirect materials costs are the costs of such materials as:

- cleaning products;
- paper and stationery;
- lubricants.

Indirect materials costs CANNOT be identified directly and in total with an item being produced.

If a material is used for different jobs, it may not be possible to identify all the costs as either direct or indirect. Let's look at an example.

Suppose you work for an organization which makes a range of timber products. One of the items is garden sheds, which are all painted. The same paint is used to decorate the factory premises.

Activity 2

2 mins

Complete the statements below with a suitable word or words.

- The paint used on the factory is _____ _____ materials cost.
- The paint used on the garden sheds is _____ _____ materials cost.

The paint used on the factory premises is **an indirect** materials cost, because it cannot be identified in total or directly with the making of sheds.

The paint used on the garden sheds is **a direct** materials cost, because it can be identified in total and directly with the making of sheds.

5 Overheads

Costs that are incurred but that are not easily identified with any particular process or product are called **overheads**. General overheads include:

- insurance of stocks of materials and finished goods, machinery and people;
- heating and lighting;
- rates.

We have already seen two other types of overhead. Wages of people not directly involved in production or directly providing a service (indirect labour) are classed as labour overheads. Examples are:

- security staff;
- maintenance fitters;
- managers and supervisors;
- secretaries and reception staff.

Indirect materials are materials overheads: safety clothing and cleaning materials are examples.

Activity 3

2 mins

Which of the following are direct and which indirect material or labour costs?

	Direct	Indirect
1. Materials used to make a particular product or provide a service.	☐	☐
2. Wages of workteams whose time is spent entirely on manufacturing or service provision.	☐	☐
3. Receptionist's salary.	☐	☐

Materials used in these ways are **direct** materials costs, and the wages of workteams whose time is spent entirely on manufacturing or service provision are **direct** labour costs. The receptionist's salary is an **indirect** labour cost or labour **overhead**.

Now let's complete our examination of cost headings with how we can collect together types of materials, labour and general overheads.

■ Factory or operations overheads.

These include general overheads, such as factory or operations centre heating, lighting, rent and rates; labour overheads, such as supervisory and reception staff; and materials overheads, such as stationery, safety clothing and cleaning materials.

■ Selling and distribution overheads.

These include general overheads such as sales office and despatch centre heating and lighting, advertising and catalogues and maintenance of cars and lorries, and labour overheads, such as sales staff commission and expenses.

■ Administration overheads.

These include accounting and financial costs, the hire of and depreciation of computers, office supplies and stationery, maintenance and depreciation of the building and its contents. They comprise a mix of materials, labour and general overheads.

Manufacturing organizations **make** things. But retail organizations are in the business of buying and selling – **trading** in other words. Insurance companies, chartered accountants and surveyors do not sell goods in any form. They sell a **service** that doesn't involve any processing of materials or selling of goods. Let's look at cost headings in such organizations.

Activity 4

Tick the relevant boxes for each classification of cost that you would expect to find in a retail organization and a service organization, respectively.

Classification of cost	Retailer	Service organization
Direct labour		
Direct materials, or goods for resale		
Shop or operations overheads		
Selling and distribution overheads		
Administration overheads		

You probably felt quite confident in ticking all three categories of overhead for both types of organization, and the goods for resale category for the retailer. But does either organization have direct labour, and does the service organization have direct materials? The answer is: yes, if they choose to do so. In other words, an organization can choose whether or not to classify items as direct or indirect, operational or overheads, depending on what it wants to achieve with its cost classifications. We shall come back to this important idea later.

Let's look first at another important way of classifying costs, not by means of their element but by their behaviour.

6 Fixed and variable costs

You will remember that we have already said that costs which vary with output are called **variable costs**. Costs which don't are called **fixed costs**.

Let's look at an example of each.

- Variable cost

  A baker sells bread in paper bags and cakes in boxes. The packaging material is directly related to the output of bread and cakes and is a **variable** cost.

- Fixed cost

  The monthly repayments of a mortgage on the baker's shop is not affected in any way by how much bread or how many cakes are sold, so this is a **fixed** cost. That doesn't necessarily mean that fixed costs don't change. Mortgage repayments can change, because interest rates change, but the reasons for the change are not related to the output of bread and cakes.

  Often, production wages are variable as they vary with output. If a hospital increases the number of patients treated, more nurses have to be taken on or extra overtime paid. Variable costs need not vary **exactly** in proportion to output or service provision. If a sudden drop in demand occurs, it's unlikely that people would immediately be laid off.

EXTENSION 1
Sometimes fixed costs can be converted to variable costs. Take a look at Kirkland's and Howard's book *Simple and Practical Costing, Pricing and Credit Control* which illustrates how this works.

Activity 5

5 mins

June Hamilton manages one of a chain of small shops. Some of the costs incurred by her shop are listed below. Some of these costs vary, depending on the amount of business June's shop does, and some stay the same, regardless of how well the business is doing.

Tick the appropriate boxes to identify costs which vary and which remain the same.

	Varies	Stays the same
Rent	☐	☐
Rates	☐	☐
Wages of sales staff	☐	☐
Wages of part-time bookkeeper	☐	☐
Commission on sales	☐	☐
Packaging material	☐	☐
Electricity for lighting and heating	☐	☐
Insurance of the property and the stock	☐	☐

I would say that rent, rates, electricity and insurance would stay the same, regardless of the amount of business June's shop does. Commission on sales and packaging materials vary depending on how much is sold. Wages stay the same in the short term but can be varied if business improves or worsens dramatically.

Costs which remain the same whether the level of business activity rises or falls are called **fixed costs**.

Costs which vary with changes in the amount of business being done are called **variable costs**.

Distinguishing between fixed and variable costs can sometimes be quite a complex issue as we have seen in the case of wages.

Now that you've examined elements of costs and how they can be classified into separate headings which may, or may not, vary with the level of activity in the workplace, we're ready to start examining ways in which we can use this information.

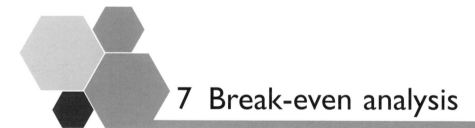

7 Break-even analysis

A simple technique called **break-even analysis** is widely used by all kinds of organizations. It allows an organization to see the minimum level of operations it must maintain to at least cover its fixed costs – its **break-even point**.

This determines the level of production and sales a business needs to break even – that is, to make no profit but no loss.

Every unit produced and sold above break-even results in profit.

Every unit produced and sold below break-even results in a loss.

To use break-even analysis to plan operations, we have to classify all costs, as we have already done, into **fixed costs** and **variable costs**.

For instance, a shop might be looking at whether it can continue in business over the summer period. All its staff have to be given at least one month's notice of dismissal. For the three month period, therefore, it would be best to treat wages as a fixed cost.

Let's see how it would work.

Unique Double Glazing expects to sell 1,000 window units at £200 each.

It expects fixed costs (rates, management salaries, machine maintenance, etc.) to be £50,000. Variable costs (materials, direct wages etc.) per window are £100 per unit.

We can anticipate the following.

■ Each window unit sold adds £200 to income but £100 to costs (the £50,000 fixed costs will exist no matter what the level of sales). The £100 surplus on each window unit sold is called **contribution per unit**.

■ When the contribution from each window unit sold matches the fixed cost, the break-even point, at which Unique makes no profit and no loss, has been reached.

In our example, we have the following:

fixed costs = £50,000

contribution per unit = £100

$$\text{break-even point} = \frac{£50,000}{£100} = 500 \text{ units}$$

If the company sells 500 units, which is 50 per cent of its target, it will have broken even. If it sells more, it will make a profit: if it sells fewer, it will make a loss.

Remember, the company expects to sell 1,000 units, and profit equals sales minus costs (both fixed and variable).

Activity 6

5 mins

Calculate the business target profit for Unique Double Glazing if expected sales are achieved.

_____

_____

_____

_____

_____

_____

I hope your calculations worked out something like this.

Sales		1,000 × £200		£200,000
Less:	Variable costs	1,000 × £100	£100,000	
	Fixed costs		£50,000	(£150,000)
Profit				£50,000

We can also express this as:

500 units above break-even × £100 (contribution) = £50,000.

Activity 7

6 mins

What will be the position if Unique Double Glazing sells:

a   600 units?

_____

_____

_____

b   400 units?

_____

_____

_____

a   If the business sells 600 units, that is 100 units more than the break-even point. The profit will then be 100 × £100 = £10,000 profit.

b   If sales only reach 400 units, that is 100 units below break-even, and the business will make a loss of 100 × £100 = £10,000 loss.

Break-even analysis is useful in helping to:

■   decide what price to charge to easily meet the break-even point and make a profit;
■   decide whether to make something yourself or to buy it in;
■   decide whether to close-down (whether to stop producing goods, provide services and so on, which do not break even).

These are major decisions, and not necessarily ones in which first line managers will become involved. We shall look at them in Session C.

So how is break-even analysis useful in practice? Well, it helps to focus the minds of everyone in the organization on the need to control costs (and generate income).

For instance, you might be manager of a newsagent, with staff costs per hour of £20. You sell *The Times* newspaper at 40p per copy. This means you have to sell 50 copies of *The Times* per hour to break even, assuming you sell nothing else and have no other costs (£20/40p). In practice, of course, you would have had to buy your stock of *The Times* from a wholesaler, so reducing the amount you make on the sale. You can see that a quiet hour or day, therefore, is money pouring down the drain.

Activity 8 ·

Identify how much it costs your organization to employ you by the hour by calculating your hourly wage rate and adding about 10% for National Insurance.

If you work in a commercial organization, work out your organization's break-even point for you in terms of sales of one of your products.

If you work in a non-profit organization, work out how much extra funding is needed so that the organization continues to make neither a profit nor a loss.

Make your notes on a separate sheet of paper.

You may find it useful from now on to think of the effects on the break-even point for your workplace of any increase in how much it pays you and how hard you work.

8 The need to control costs

It's sometimes difficult to decide which costs are fixed and which variable. In the longer term, virtually nothing is fixed. We usually regard business rates, for example, as a fixed cost as they are a payment demanded by the local authority, and outside the control of the business. But rates vary between one town and another, and may increase or decrease from year to year. A business can reduce its rates bill. It can move!

Fixed costs are fixed over a period of time, and that timescale is linked to the scale of decision making that takes place in the organization. For instance, a power generator has to make very long-term plans. It is not easy to move a power station! But the situation for an employment agency is far more fluid. On a day-to-day level, the important distinction we have to make is between the costs we can control and those we cannot.

Activity 9 · 2 mins

Tick the costs below that you think you can influence at work.

Large airlines use a 'hub and spoke' model to spread high fixed servicing costs over many aircraft. All flights go to a hub airport where there are flights to hundreds of possible final destinations (spokes).

■ Quarterly electricity cost. ☐

■ Rent of the firm's premises. ☐

■ Rental cost of each telephone line. ☐

■ Quarterly cost of telephone calls. ☐

The cost of electricity and telephone calls made can be kept down by your own efforts.

Perhaps you feel, particularly if you work for a large organization, that the amount of electricity you use or how many telephone calls you make doesn't make any real difference on the overall total.

To some extent you're right. If you turn off lights when you go out of a room or make a shorter telephone call it will make a difference of only a few pounds a quarter. But by setting an example to your workteam you can encourage your team members to control costs. You will also exert quite a bit of influence on other people who come into your work area, if they see that you take cost control seriously.

As a general rule, variable costs are more likely to be within your control than fixed costs, and it is these which you can most easily help to keep down by your own efforts.

What can we do about other costs which are not directly within the control of the people involved?

Let's take an example of your workteam's time. How much they are paid and their pay scale is probably outside your control. But you can make sure that value for money is obtained for that cost.

Activity 10

S/NVQs B1.1, B1.2

This Activity may provide the basis of evidence for your S/NVQ portfolio. If you are intending to take this course of action, it might be better to write your answers on separate sheets of paper.

Jot down **one** way in which you can ensure that you get 'value for money' for the cost of your workteam's time. Make a note of ways in which you can implement your suggestion.

_____

_____

_____

Perhaps you said something like 'keep them working', or 'make efficient use of their time', or even 'manage them properly'. You may have started to think in detail about selecting the right people for the job and training them properly. Perhaps you could draw up a time schedule for yourself and your team.

Now look at this example.

Activity 11

2 mins

Shari's workteam uses computer screens which are linked to a large computer at head office. Frequently they spend long, frustrating periods in front of the screen waiting for responses from the heavily loaded computer. Response time is slow and seems to be getting worse. She is able to use her workteam's time on other jobs so that their time isn't wasted so much, but the real problem doesn't go away. What can she do?

Write down one suggestion.

_____

_____

_____

_____

She could try a number of possibilities, for example:

■ ring head office and try to find out what the problem is;
■ talk to her manager about it and get him or her to take it up.

If Shari was to report 'a general feeling' that response time is getting worse, it may not meet with much reaction. It would be more helpful if she kept a record of the problems and noted exactly what was happening.

In any situation, and equipped with some real evidence, you can:

■ identify the scale of the problem yourself;
■ convince your manager that you have a problem which you cannot solve on your own.

We'll look at this in detail later in the workbook.

To sum up, we can say that you can tackle problems of costs on three fronts:

■ keep down costs which are within your control;
■ get value for money for costs which you can't control directly;
■ keep records of cost problems which you have identified but can't influence without support.

Self-assessment 1

10 mins

1 Identify the differences between direct and indirect materials costs.

_____

_____

_____

2 Claire runs a local newspaper. She pays her advertising sales staff on a commission-only basis and her reporters are given a weekly wage. Are the different forms of wage fixed or variable costs?

■ the wages of the advertising sales staff are _____ _____ ;

■ the wages of the reporters are _____ _____ .

3 Fill in the missing words in the following sentences.

a Direct labour costs _____ be _____ identified with a particular product.

b Wages which _____ be identified with a particular product are _____ labour costs.

c Direct labour costs are often _____ costs because they increase or decrease in proportion to the production being carried out.

4 The Feelgood Health Club has weekly fixed costs of £18,000 per week. There are no variable costs. Each member pays £15 per week to be a member. What is Feelgood's break-even number of members?

5 Sam is a first line manager in a factory assembling PCs. Tick the costs which would be under Sam's control and those which would not.

	Controllable	Not controllable
■ wastage of components used in the production of PCs	☐	☐
■ advertising costs of PCs	☐	☐
■ Sam's basic salary	☐	☐

Answers to these questions can be found on page 100.

8 Summary

- Profit = Sales − Costs.

- Costs are broadly made up of **labour costs**, **materials costs** and **overheads**.

- Labour costs have to be divided into:

  - direct labour costs – which can be totally identified with time spent making a particular product or providing a service;
  - indirect labour costs – which are identified with work other than making a product or directly providing a service.

- Materials costs, like labour costs, have to be divided into direct and indirect materials costs.

- Costs that relate to supporting the main activity are called overheads. Overheads can include indirect materials and labour, depending on how the organization classifies its costs

- Costs can be identified as:

  - **variable** – varying with output;
  - **fixed** – incurred regardless of output.

- Each unit an organization sells makes a contribution to fixed costs of its selling price less its variable costs of production An organization breaks even when its fixed costs are covered by its total contribution. If it sells more it makes a profit; if it sells less it makes a loss.

- The break-even point, at which an organization makes neither a profit nor a loss, is calculated as fixed costs/contribution per unit.

- To control costs:

  - continually monitor and minimize costs within your control;
  - get value for money from costs you cannot directly control;
  - keep records of costs you cannot control without support.

Session B
Standard costing

1 Introduction

You know that it is useful to control costs. But how do you know you are controlling the right ones? And by how much should you reduce them, if possible? You can switch lights off and turn down the heating, but your workteam are unlikely to work well in the cold and dark.

It helps you to control anything – the output of a machine or a workteam, for instance – if there is a standard against which to measure performance.

In cost control, the first step is to decide what the costs should be and then control what happens in such a way that you meet those 'target' costs. If actual costs of the operation turn out to be different from the expected figure, then you look at the differences – called variances – and find out why they are different. Then you can decide what action should be taken to bring them back to target.

In this session we will look at different standards and how to use them to control costs.

2 Setting standards

Standard costs are concerned with individual units of production or service. Each item of production or service, for instance, will have a standard cost.

A standard cost is a predetermined cost that is achieved by setting standards related to particular circumstances or conditions of work.

> Costs change over time, so standards should be reviewed regularly to ensure that they are still relevant.

A standard cost should indicate not just what a particular cost is **expected** to be, but also what it **ought** to be under certain conditions.

You can apply standard costs to all the costs in the workplace. These may include:

- direct labour;
- direct materials;
- overheads (fixed and variable).

A mechanic may, for example, be expected to complete the servicing of a car in an hour and this will involve one hour's direct labour cost plus a direct materials cost for, say, oil filter, lubricants and other replacement parts.

2.1 Standard cost rates

Standard cost rates are estimated by taking all sorts of considerations into account.

Activity 12

a Jot down **two** things which you would take into account in estimating materials costs for something which will be used extensively in your workplace for the next year.

_____

_____

b Write down **two** matters you would have to take into account in estimating labour costs for a forthcoming period.

_____

_____

I hope you have thought of taking the following into account in respect of materials costs:

- the purchase price;
- any expected change in price (for instance, you might know that the price of oil or floppy disks was going to increase);
- any discount you could negotiate.

The following factors, among others, would be relevant for labour costs:

- the current hourly rate/piece rate;
- likely agreements on pay rises;
- other costs, such as overtime premiums, bonuses, employer's National Insurance contributions, pension contributions.

Deciding on how much things ought to cost is only one side of the question. The other matter to consider is how many of the things in question should be used for each unit of production or service. In other words, we need to decide how well production will perform.

So now let's look at performance standard rates.

2.2 Standard performance rates

To use a standard costing system, somebody must decide:

- the quantities, types and mix of materials to produce any given product;
- the amount and type of labour to produce any given product or service.

These technical standards are usually set by specialists and involve techniques such as method study and job evaluation.

Two types of standard are commonly used:

- ideal standards;
- expected standards.

Ideal standards are based on perfect working conditions. However, conditions are seldom perfect, often for reasons outside our immediate control. Ideal standards can help to highlight major variances, but people tend to find them rather discouraging, because the targets may be too high.

Much better, usually, are **expected standards**. These could well be called realistic standards, as they build in an allowance for an acceptable level of inefficiency. If the workteam is well managed and willing to co-operate, expected standards should be attainable.

Activity 13 · 5 mins

| S/NVQs B1.1, B1.2 |

This Activity may provide the basis of appropriate evidence for your S/NVQ portfolio. If you are intending to take this course of action, it might be better to write your answers on separate sheets of paper.

Identify three causes for breaks in production or delivery of service which are not planned and which your workteam has experienced. Suggest changes that you could recommend to your manager to address such situations.

_____

_____

_____

_____

_____

_____

Certain planned breaks are important to allow staff to eat and rest physically and mentally. They are often required by law, say in the case of lorry drivers and uses of VDUs. There are, though, breaks that can occur unexpectedly, such as:

- when equipment breaks down. A hairdresser may have spare cutting equipment to call upon but if a baker's oven breaks down, replacement may not be possible. A rapid service and repair contract is essential.
- where the organization runs out of stock and production ceases. Plans for alternative work so that employees have something to do would avoid unnecessary costs, or alternative stockholding policies could be employed.
- when accidents or injuries occur. Good health and safety training and procedures should limit this problem.

2.3 Standard costing and non-manufacturing organizations

A full standard costing system is less common in organizations that provide a service rather than manufacture something. Many industries, nevertheless, find it useful to set performance standards in order to:

a base costs upon them, and then;

b measure actual performance.

For example, a building contractor might base costs on performance standards for:

■ cubic metres of earth excavated per hour by a mechanical digger;
■ lorry loads of earth shifted per day;
■ bricks laid per hour.

Activity 14

3 mins

In an office you may find sales order processing clerks, and administrators sending letters in response to queries at work. Also the manager may spend a lot of time talking to clients in a separate office.

Suggest two possible performance standards which you could set if you were in charge in this situation.

_____

_____

You could set performance standards for:

■ letters created per hour by an administrator;
■ percentage completion of correct invoices by the sales order processing clerks;
■ number of deals by the manager per day.

3 Standard costing in practice

Let's look first at a very simple example.

Karl makes large, luxury cages for pet rats. He knows that each cage requires 6 square metres of wire mesh, and 12 metres of timber. It takes him 3.5 hours to make a cage. Wire mesh costs £2 per square metre, and timber costs £1.50

per metre. He pays himself £15 per hour. What is the standard cost for each cage?

We can calculate this by drawing up a standard cost statement. Make sure you can trace every item in the figure below to the information above, and that you can follow through the calculations.

Standard cost statement: Rat cage

		Quantity used	Rate £	Standard cost £
Direct materials				
	Wire mesh	6	2.00	12.00
	Timber	12	1.50	18.00
Direct labour				
	Karl's time	3.5	15.00	52.50
Standard cost per cage				82.50

Once you are happy that you understand the way in which this standard cost statement is constructed, you can put standard costing into operation in the following Activity.

Activity 15

5 mins

Plastiform plc makes a range of plastic furniture. A standard costing system is in operation. The following information is available for one product – plastic tables.

The raw material (plastic) has been costed at £6.10 per metre. The standard usage of material is reckoned to be 5 metres per table.

Two types of labour are required in the production process: moulders and cutters.

- The standard rate for moulders is £8.00 per hour.
- The standard rate for cutters is £10.00 per hour.
- The expected standard for moulders is 1½ hours per table.
- The expected standard for cutters is 2½ hours per table.

Complete the standard cost statement below to show what the standard cost will be for a table.

Standard cost statement: plastic table

Direct materials: 5 metres at £6.10   = £_____

Direct wages:

Moulder _____ hours × £_____ = £6.00

Cutter _____ hours × £_____ = _____

_____

The answer to this Activity can be found on page 102.

The system an organization uses to analyse and ultimately to control its costs can be as simple or as complicated as the organization wishes. Karl and Plastiform plc produce standard cost statements just for direct materials and labour. What about overheads?

We saw in Session A that an organization can classify its costs in various ways, in particular in relation to:

- which costs are treated as direct costs and which as indirect;
- which costs are treated as what type of overhead.

This is important, since a standard costing system can identify a certain amount of overhead to each unit of production or service if the organization sees fit, as well as direct materials and labour.

Activity 16

3 mins

Karl has also worked out that, for each hour he works on the rat cages, he incurs rent, rates, heating and insurance costs of £3. Remember he works for three and a half hours on each cage. By how much will the standard cost per cage rise if he takes overheads into account?

I hope you calculated that the standard cost will rise by £3.50 × 3 = £10.50 so the total standard cost will be £93.00.

Now let's see how differences between actual costs and standard costs (**variances**) can be calculated and analysed.

4 Variances from standard

Variances are the differences between what costs **actually are** and what they **should be** – the standard.

A variance can be either **adverse** (when the actual cost is higher than the standard) or **favourable** (when the cost is actually lower than the standard).

With a basic standard costing system, variances can be highlighted for:

■ every material used;
■ every type of direct labour;
■ variable overheads (such as workshop heat and light).

Clearly, this detailed information is very important to managers who wish to control work. Notice that we are only looking here at the costs that fluctuate with levels of activity. These are the ones that are most likely to be controllable by first line managers.

The following diagram shows how an analysis of these work variances breaks down.

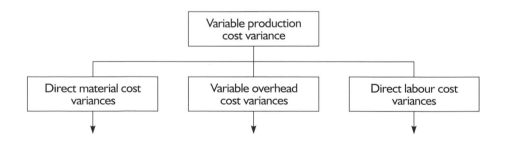

We shall use an analysis of materials and labour costs to illustrate that standard costing can help pinpoint variances and so improve control.

4.1 Direct material cost variances

Direct material cost variances can be divided into two types:

- usage variance;
- price variance.

Don't worry about the terminology too much. We have already seen the usage rate when we said that Karl uses 12 metres of timber. The price rate was £1.50 per metre.

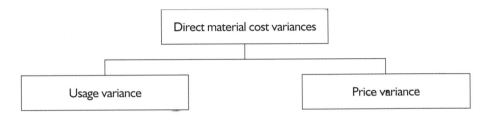

If an adverse usage variance occurs, it means that more material has been used than the standard indicated. This might have come about because inefficient methods meant that more scrap than expected was produced.

Activity 17

A decision to improve a price variance by using cheaper materials can lead to more scrap and a worsening usage variance. The consequences of changes made in response to variances need careful consideration.

Who do you think is ultimately responsible for a usage variance?

_____

Who do you think is directly responsible for excessive scrap being produced?

_____

Ultimately, the production controller, or similarly named person, is responsible for a variance from standard usage. However, the first line manager is likely to have to account directly for scrap being higher than expected.

Now let's look at the direct labour cost variance.

4.2 Direct labour cost variances

Direct labour cost variances break down to:

- efficiency variance;
- idle time variance;
- rate variance.

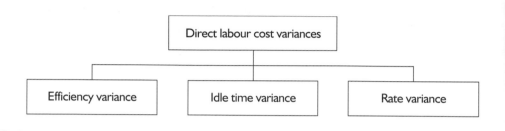

An adverse **efficiency** variance means that the workteam spent longer making the product than the standard indicated. So, for instance, Karl spent 4 hours making a cage. Once again, we would need to know who was responsible and the reasons for the standard not being achieved.

An **idle time** variance is caused by the workteam not having any work for a longer period than expected.

This could be caused, among other reasons, by:

- equipment breakdown;
- materials hold-up;
- a lack of power.

Activity 18

2 mins

Suggest who or what you think would be responsible for each of these causes of an adverse idle time variance.

Equipment breakdown _____

Materials hold-up _____

Lack of power_____

EXTENSION 2
Calculating variances can be time-consuming. Computerization is used to provide us with variance information. This extension shows how a spreadsheet can be used to help with costing materials, labour and overheads in Sue Nugus' book, *Financial Planning using Spreadsheets*.

In practice, things are often more complicated than they seem. There could be a number of contributory factors which different managers would have to account for. It's quite possible that you have suggested:

- for equipment breakdown, the maintenance engineer;
- for materials hold-up, the stock control department;
- for lack of power, interruption of power supply owing to adverse weather conditions.

An adverse **rate** variance means that the workteam costs for the time taken were more than was expected. This is most often because overtime has had to be paid, say because other work overran its time in a factory and so work had to be completed outside normal factory hours. Usually the production controller is responsible for this.

Another common cause of a labour rate variance is the use of more highly paid staff than was anticipated.

4.3 Calculating and presenting variances

Now that we have looked at the nature of variances and at some of their possible causes, we shall briefly calculate some simple variances and try to identify their significance.

Activity 19 · 10 mins

Despite Karl's careful preparation of a standard cost statement for the rat cages, he has now found that it has cost him £83.40 to produce one. He has used 12.5 metres of timber, which cost £20, and 7 square metres of wire mesh, which cost £15.40. He took four hours to make the cage. To try to save money, Karl paid himself only £48.00 for those four hours.

Fill in the variance statement below, in order to identify the causes of the total cost variance (the details have been filled in, and the calculation of the actual rate made, for the wire mesh).

Variance statement: Rat cage

	Quantity planned	Rate planned £	Standard cost (A) £	Quantity used	Actual rate £	Actual cost (B) £	Variance (A – B) £
Direct materials							
Wire mesh	6	2.00	12.00	7	2.20	15.40	3.40 (A)
Timber	12	1.50	18.00				
Direct labour							
Karl's time	3.5	15.00	52.50				
Standard cost			82.50		Actual cost		

You should have produced a statement like this.

Variance statement: Rat cage

	Quantity planned	Rate planned £	Standard cost (A) £	Quantity used	Actual rate £	Actual cost (B) £	Variance (A – B) £
Direct materials							
Wire mesh	6	2.00	12.00	7	2.20	15.40	3.40 (A)
Timber	12	1.50	18.00	12.5	1.60	20.00	2.00 (A)
Direct labour							
Karl's time	3.5	15.00	52.50	4	12.00	48.00	4.50 (F)
Standard cost			82.50		Actual cost	83.40	0.90 (A)

For each type of material, and for labour, we can break the variances down further to see exactly what the causes were (we know that there was no idle time).

Detailed variance statement: Rat cage

£

Wire mesh price variance	(7 metres × £0.20)	1.40 (A)	
Wire mesh usage variance	(1 × £2.00)	2.00 (A)	
Wire mesh variance (adverse)			£3.40 (A)
Timber price variance	(12.5 metres × £0.10)	1.25 (A)	
Timber usage variance	(0.5 metres × £1.50)	0.75 (A)	
Timber variance (adverse)			£2.00 (A)
Labour rate variance	(4 hours × £3.00)	12.00 (F)	
Labour efficiency variance	(0.5 hours × £15.00)	7.50 (A)	
Labour variance (favourable)			£4.50 (F)
Total cost variance			£0.90 (A)

Don't worry too much about how these detailed variances were calculated. What this statement shows us is what we intuitively knew already: Karl used more materials, and paid more for them per metre, than he expected, and also took longer than he expected to make the cage. By calculating these detailed variances, however, we have pinpointed and quantified the causes, and can then set about ways of reducing those variances that are unacceptable to Karl.

5 The value of standard costing

Standard costing, largely controlled by people, means that a lot of information about performance is gathered.

This leads us to two other advantages of standard costing:

- it's possible to achieve real economies through thinking in advance about the best materials to use, the best methods and so on;
- attention can be concentrated on the variances that **exceed** predetermined limits, rather than looking at all variances, some of which may be quite minor.

So an analysis of variances from standard costs can lead to a very detailed and far-reaching investigation of the problem. Perhaps you've already been involved in such investigations.

Identifying the responsible people is not a witch hunt; we are not looking for somebody to blame. The important step is to account for the variance so that better control can be established in future.

Self-assessment 2 · 15 mins

1   Complete the following definition by filling in the missing words.

A standard cost is a _____ cost that is achieved by setting _____ related to particular circumstances or conditions of work.

2   Identify two reasons for setting performance standards in any organization.

_____

_____

3   Calculate the standard cost of a vase using the following information:

- glass is used which costs £8.00 per metre; a quarter of a metre is used for one vase;
- a glassworker is paid £7.50 per hour and can make ten vases in an hour.

> **Standard cost statement**
>
> Direct materials: _____
>
> Direct wages: _____
>
> _____

4   Identify the variances comprising:

■ direct material cost variances

_____

_____

■ direct labour cost variances

_____

_____

5   State what is indicated by favourable and adverse variances.

_____

_____

_____

_____

Answers to these questions can be found on pages 100–1.

5 Summary

- A standard cost is a cost calculated in advance and based on certain approved, specified work practices.

- Standard costing allows management to pinpoint variances precisely.

- Standard costs have two elements:

  - costs;
  - performance level.

- Standard performance levels should be based on expected standards and contain an allowable level of slack.

- Analysis of cost variances can lead to better cost control.

- The complete diagram of variances we have discussed is as shown below:

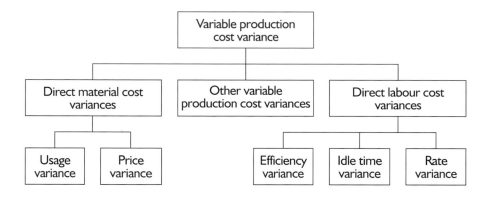

Session C
Controlling and reducing costs

1 Introduction

There are two main ways of controlling costs: effective monitoring (for which good information is needed) and active control. In this session we shall look first at how information can be collected and used, so that the person who controls costs is involved in monitoring them, and thus becomes highly cost-conscious.

Once costs have been collected (in cost units and cost centres), variances can be calculated. Most organizations accept that some level of variance is inevitable. However, at some point an adverse variance becomes unacceptable, and its adverse effects must be reduced. The first line manager may then be called upon to take more active control measures.

Sometimes a first line manager may be called on to reduce costs in a cost-cutting exercise. This is a more extreme form of cost control, which we shall also look at here.

Let's begin by looking at a few decisions in which cost information is very important.

2 Cost information and decisions

Consider the following Activity.

Activity 20 · 6 mins

Below are three questions on cost. For each one, jot down what you think would be the kind of decision that will be made as a result of the question being answered.

■ How many units of a proposed new product are likely to be sold, and what are the fixed costs? Once this question is answered, you would use the information to help you decide

_____

_____

■ How much does it cost to feed a patient in hospital for a week (a) using the hospital kitchen, (b) using an outside caterer? The answer to this question might lead the hospital authorities to investigate

_____

_____

_____

■ Can gas from a certain field be sold at more or less than the cost of extracting it? No further changes to working practices are possible. The answer to this question might lead to

_____

_____

_____

In the first instance, by knowing the fixed costs and a good estimation of likely sales, you can work out how the fixed costs can be spread over each unit sold. This will help in setting a price per unit to provide a profit. This is a pricing decision, based on break-even analysis.

In the second instance, hospital authorities can investigate whether it is cheaper to use their own kitchens and staff or to buy in the services of an outside caterer. There may well be things other than costs, such as the need to meet specific dietary needs or deal with rapidly changing volumes of patients, which affect the decision. This is a 'make or buy' decision.

Finally, gas fields in which the costs of extraction exceed the selling price are closed down because they are unprofitable. As with the earlier decisions, costs will not be the only things looked at, but they will be important. This is a closure decision.

The three kinds of decision we have looked at – pricing, 'make or buy' and closure – are major decisions made in a wide range of industries. Without collecting information about costs on a regular basis, organizations may not even know whether a particular process makes a profit or runs at a loss, or whether it would be cheaper for them to make something themselves or buy it in. Costs and cost information are therefore important to managers making a wide range of decisions.

2.1 Basic cost statements

A cost statement is often used to show the breakdown of costs so that the final cost of a product or service can be analysed.

Let's begin by looking at a manufacturing example. It's helpful in manufacturing to identify another cost: the **total factory cost**. This includes all the **prime** or direct costs plus all the indirect costs arising out of the need to keep the factory (but not the offices) running. Indirect costs are **factory overheads**.

Activity 21   10 mins

Write down one example of an appropriate cost beside each item shown in the following cost statement for the production of a car. I've given examples of factory overheads to help.

Cost statement of a car

	£	£	Example of appropriate cost
Direct material		2,500	
Direct labour		2,500	
Prime cost		5,000	
Factory overheads		3,500	Production line, lighting, heating,
Total factory cost		8,500	health and safety expenditure
Administrative overheads	1,000		
Selling and distribution overheads (including dealer's profit margin)	1,500	2,500	
Total costs		11,000	
Profit		1,000	
Selling price		£12,000	

You could have thought of all sorts of things, since the manufacture, selling and distribution of a car is a complex process involving many people.

Under the prime cost heading, you could have identified any of the raw materials that go into a car and the wages of anybody directly involved in production.

Administration could be anything to do with purchasing, payments, stock control or any of the paperwork involved in running a business.

Selling and distribution would include advertising, promotions, delivering cars to the dealers and getting them in showroom condition.

Now let's see how this sort of analysis can be used if we adapt it slightly for an organization, such as a hospital, which provides a service.

We'll say it costs about £600 a week to keep a patient in a general ward in hospital.

Cost structure of patient care on general ward
(cost per in-patient week)

	£	£	Examples
Direct labour		250	Medical and nursing salaries
Direct materials		100	Drugs, medical supplies
Prime cost		350	
Administrative overheads	100		Clerical salaries, rates, telephone
General hospital overheads	150	250	Catering, cleaning costs and maintenance
Total costs		£600	

Once again, the costs are broken down into direct costs and overheads.

2.2 Cost units

Costs can be divided into direct costs and overheads. However, this analysis is only useful if the costs relate to an identifiable item, called a *cost unit*. In the example of the cost of producing a car, the car was the cost unit. In the case of the hospital, it was an in-patient week. Each organization defines its own cost units.

The most obvious cost unit is the finished product. For instance, a brewery may send out its beer in barrels or kegs which would be the cost units. A cement factory will probably send its cement out by the tonne, so will probably use a tonne of cement as a cost unit.

Cost units can be used by organizations that provide a service too.

Activity 22 ·

4 mins

Jot down what you think might be the cost units used by:

■ swimming baths

_____

■ a school canteen

_____

■ letter delivery at Royal Mail

_____

Swimming baths would probably use a bather as a cost unit. A school canteen could use individual meals produced as a cost unit. Royal Mail is a more difficult problem. You could have suggested an individual letter or package for the sorting office, or an individual address for delivery staff.

In fact, a business can analyse any part of the workplace and work out appropriate cost units. For example, some of the cost units we might find in a car factory are:

■ final product – cost per car;
■ electricity cost – cost per kilowatt hour the production line is running;
■ computer running cost – cost per computer minute of operation;
■ canteen – cost per canteen meal.

In a complex organization, analysing costs at a more detailed level like this will help the people responsible for those costs to monitor them, and take action if necessary.

This leads us to the subject of cost centres.

3 Cost centres

A cost centre is a location where costs can be identified, grouped together and then finally related to a cost unit.

A cost centre is, in other words, a collection point for costs.

By a 'location' I mean something like:

- a department within a particular workplace;
- a work area;
- a machine or group of machines;
- a person, e.g. a hospital consultant.

The advantages of breaking down costs and collecting them in a number of cost centres are that:

- information on costs can be collected more easily;
- information on costs in different parts of the organization can be provided;
- managers of particular cost centres can be given standards against which costs can be controlled.

Identifying costs in cost centres helps to control costs in the various parts of the organization, and to control how each unit or department spends money.

The diagram below shows an example of three cost centres within an organization. Each cost centre collects:

- costs of materials and labour used within the centre;
- a proportion of the overheads for the whole organization.

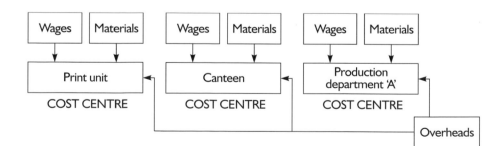

Collection of costs in cost centres

Activity 23

3 mins

Look at the diagram on the previous page and decide into which cost centres you would collect the following costs:

Paper for digital print machine _____

Cook's wages _____

Wages of machine operator working in Department A _____

It looks as though paper for the digital print machine is a print unit cost; the cook's wages are a canteen cost; and the machine operator's wages are a cost incurred in production Department A. Each cost centre would collect the costs relevant to it.

The canteen and the print unit are providing a service to other parts of the organization. So we can distinguish between two types of cost centre:

■ service centres, and
■ product centres.

An important aim of a manufacturing organization is to make goods; that's how it earns its income. All services (such as the canteen, the stores, the maintenance department and so on) exist only to assist in that aim. Therefore, all costs must be finally transferred from the service centres to the product centres. The total costs of the product centre will then be spread over the cost units it produces.

For a building firm, the total cost of building houses is made up of many different individual costs. If the firm provides safety helmets for its workers, the cost of the helmets may be initially part of the materials costs for a 'safety department' cost centre. Ultimately these costs must appear in the cost of each house, the cost unit.

You may be thinking that this process sounds rather complicated and difficult to manage. It is, if it is not organized properly. Collecting costs is a detailed process that can only be done effectively by using cost codes for every item of cost. It is very often the role of the first line manager to ensure that the correct cost codes are created and used. So let's look at them now.

3.1 Cost codes

A good cost system enables costs to be:

- collected;
- analysed;
- controlled.

This means that we have to be able to find out precisely what expenses have been incurred in any part of the workplace, and we have to know how much we are spending in the workplace as a whole on different sorts of expense (overtime, electricity, stationery, etc.).

To help us do this a system of cost codes is often used. This will mean having two types of code:

- a special code for each cost centre, which will identify any costs incurred in that cost centre;
- a special code for each type of cost – such as stationery – wherever it occurs throughout the workplace.

By combining the cost centre code (for the accounts department, for example) and the code identifying the type of cost (stationery), we can identify how much has been spent on any particular item in any particular cost centre, and so control costs throughout the organization.

Let's look at how a cost coding system works.

Each workplace uses certain groups of numbers to mean particular things. These groups usually contain enough spare numbers for new kinds of cost to be added to the list of codes. For instance, a workplace with seven different cost centres may allocate the group of codes 01, 02, 03, . . ., 18, 19 to cost centres, providing plenty of room to expand the list.

Let's look at a selection of likely cost codes for a general hospital.

Hospital cost centres	Codes	Items of expenditure	Codes
Ward 1	001	Ward sister's salary	025
Ward 2	002	Staff nurse's salary	026
Ward 3	003	Cleaner's wages	107
Theatre 1	098	Medical equipment	400–449
Theatre 2	099	Drugs	450–500
Pharmacy	171	Laundry assistant's wages	181
Physiotherapy department	264	Cleaning materials	600–630
Laundry	351	Cook's wages	197
Canteen	400		

Sister's salary on Ward 2 will be coded 002 025. Cleaning materials for Ward 3 could be coded 003 610 or 003 622 or 003 630, because the range indicates different codes for different types of cleaning material.

Activity 24 · 5 mins

Cost codes must be clear and well understood for them to be effective. A code for 'sundry expenses' is often overused.

Work out codes for the following. Where you have a range of numbers, choose any one from within that range.

■ Theatre 1 staff nurse's salary _____ _____

■ Theatre 2 medical equipment _____ _____

■ Physiotherapy department medical equipment _____ _____

■ Drug coded 459 and ordered for the pharmacy _____ _____

■ Canteen cook's wages _____ _____

The answer to this Activity can be found on page 102.

Activity 25 · 2 mins

Here is a list of some costs in the hospital to which cost codes have been allocated. One of them seems rather suspicious and would need to be checked out. (Tick the suspect code.)

098 107   ☐

001 026   ☐

400 457   ☐

According to these cost codes, the canteen has been ordering drugs (400 457)! This sounds very worrying and needs investigating urgently.

What this activity shows us is that information on costs is not only used to help us minimize costs – it also helps to make sure that costs are only occurred where they should be.

A system of cost codes means that everybody in the workplace describes each kind of cost in the same way. Information about costs is simplified and is presented in a standard way, making it easier to interpret and analyse.

Cost codes, made up of cost centre code and type of cost code, also mean that every single cost can be traced to a certain cost centre, improving control.

Identifying certain kinds of expense by the same code throughout the workplace means that you can also see how much you are spending on certain things (overtime or electricity, for instance), overall. This will help in deciding how best to utilize resources, to minimize expenditure or to reduce total costs.

4 Control through cost centres

Whether the cost centre is a work area, a machine or a group of machines or a team of people, it could well be you, as first line manager, who is responsible for maintaining the cost centre and controlling the associated costs.

You might have to:

■ requisition materials (materials);
■ authorize and collect time sheets (labour);
■ control the level of overhead costs in your work area, such as electricity or telephone use.

Let's look at how materials and wages costs are collected in appropriate cost centres.

The collection and application of overhead costs is rather more complex, but we'll look at that later.

4.1 Cost centres and materials costs

A first line manager may have the responsibility for:

■ raising a materials requisition for goods in the workplace stores which are needed for the job;

■ raising a purchase requisition for goods needed for the job, which are not in the stores and so have to be specially bought;

■ taking care of materials once they are in the work area.

The diagram below shows an outline of the movement of paperwork and goods which take place when items are requested. The sharp-edged boxes denote paperwork, and the round-edged boxes denote locations.

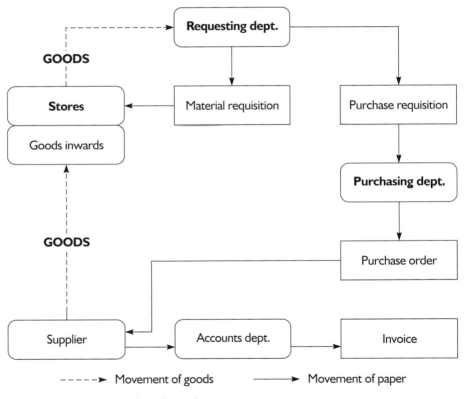

Movement of paperwork and goods

Activity 26 · 10 mins

Look at Figure 2 and identify three people or departments, apart from the requesting department and the supplier, who have a part to play in the materials costing system.

Against each one write down briefly what you think their responsibilities are.

_____

_____

_____

_____

_____

Here is my breakdown of the roles played by various departments in the materials costing system.

- Purchasing department/purchasing officer:
  - ordering goods;
  - keeping lists of approved suppliers;
  - checking suppliers' prices.

- Goods inward department:
  - receiving goods;
  - checking quality and quantity of goods supplied;
  - issuing goods-received notes to accounts department.

- Stores department:
  - storage and care of goods in store;
  - keeping records of receipts and issues to and from stores and current balances of items held;
  - issuing purchase requisitions when stock levels fall;
  - issuing supplies for certain jobs on receipt of a proper materials requisition note.

- Accounting department:
  - receiving and checking invoices against orders and goods received notes;
  - keeping accounting records for the entire workplace;
  - paying the supplier;
  - costing materials for particular jobs;
  - recording cost information.

Activity 27

5 mins

Look back at Session B on standard costing. How do you think a standard cost statement for making a particular item or providing a particular service would help a first line manager in requesting materials and controlling their cost?

_____

_____

_____

I hope you can see that a standard cost statement helps the practical process in at least two ways. First, the manager can see what items are needed for a product or service, such as wire mesh and timber for a rat cage. Secondly, the manager can see how much they are expecting to pay for that material.

Without this sort of information, the materials requisition might just as well say: 'enough stuff to make a rat cage, and hang the expense!'

4.2 Cost centres and labour costs

You are likely to be directly involved in the control and recording of labour costs. Your position gives you a degree of authority over your workteam and responsibility for:

■ controlling timekeeping, particularly important if you are monitoring a flexi-time system;
■ controlling quality of performance;
■ recording time spent on individual jobs, if applicable;
■ passing time records to the appropriate department for analysis.

Other departments which will be involved to some extent in the labour costing system are:

■ wages department;
■ accounts department;
■ personnel department.

Time sheets or similar forms to record time spent at work are used to help in the calculation of labour costs.

Time Sheet							
Name *A Brown* Department (cost centre) *Assembly shop*						Employee no. *740* Grade: *M* Week ending *25/6*	
	AM		PM		Excess hours		
Date	In	Out	In	Out	In	Out	Total hours
21/6	7.58	12.01	1.00	5.01			8.00
22/6	7.55	12.00	1.00	5.05			8.00
23/6	8.00	12.00	1.00	5.00	6.00	9.00	11.00
24/6	7.55	12.00	1.00	4.55			8.00
25/6	7.59	12.01	1.02	5.00			8.00

The time sheet, illustrated above, has to be analysed before being passed to the wages department.

Activity 28 · 5 mins

Using the information on the time sheet, fill in the blank spaces below, assuming a normal working week of 40 hours.

Regular time _____ hours at £6.00   £ _____

Overtime   _____ hours at £9.00   £ _____

Gross earnings   £ _____

The answer to this Activity can be found on page 102.

The first line manager is usually directly responsible for confirming that the records of how much time the workteam has spent are true. In a flexi-time system, appropriate core time must be confirmed (i.e. employees should be at work when required) as well as attending for the appropriate total time within the flexible working pattern. But the team leader's responsibilities for labour cost control don't end here.

Typical additional responsibilities would include:

- allocating time to individual jobs;
- allocating an appropriate grade of staff to a particular job;
- controlling the amount of time spent on individual jobs by each member of the workteam;
- keeping idle time, such as travel time, to a minimum.

I hope you can see that knowing how much time should be spent by what kinds of staff, and how much that time should cost, will be useful to the manager in performing these tasks. As with materials, this information will come from the standard cost card.

To the practical responsibilities we can add the 'paperwork responsibilities' which go with the job:

- confirming that cost details shown for each job are correct;
- passing costs per job to the accounts department for analysis;
- verifying idle time costs;
- passing details of idle time costs to the accounts department so that it can be properly accounted for. (Generally it needs to be apportioned on some reasonable basis over all jobs).

> Cost control is only worthwhile if it saves more for an organization than the costs of its operation. Too much time or paperwork and you should question its relevance.

A computer report which analyses time and services provided, is normally the key document in transferring labour cost information from a particular work area to whoever is responsible for summarizing cost information.

Activity 29 · 5 mins

A Brown, whose time sheet we saw in Activity 28, spent the whole of Monday, Tuesday and Wednesday starting and completing the assembly of Product X.

Fill in the actual labour cost for Product X on the computer report below. What does the comparison against the expected cost tell you?

PRODUCT X

Assembly costs

Grade of labour used:	Actual cost M	Expected cost N	
Regular time:	___ hours at £_____	22 hours at £7.50	165.00
Overtime:	___ hours at £_____	0	0.00
Total assembly labour:			£165.00

The comparison against expected cost tells me

_____

_____

You should have come up with the following calculation.

PRODUCT X

Assembly costs

	Actual cost		Expected cost	
Grade of labour used:	M		N	
Regular time:	24 hours at £6.00	144.00	22 hours at £7.50	165.00
Overtime:	3 hours at £9.00	27.00	0	0.00
Total assembly labour:		£171.00		£165.00

I hope you can see that the cost has exceeded what was expected. This was because a lower grade of employee was used, who spent more time than was expected, including overtime.

How could the first line manager have controlled this overrun of costs? It depends on the circumstances. Perhaps a grade N employee was not available, or was sick. If so, the manager needs to consider reworking the work schedules so that the right numbers of the right grades of staff are always available. Perhaps training could be implemented to upgrade the grade M staff.

Alternatively, the situation may have been outside the manager's control. Product X might have been planned to arrive when grade N staff were available, but have been delayed by another department.

Now that we have raised the issue of control, let's have a look for a moment at the question of idle time.

Common causes are:

■ equipment breakdown;
■ power failure;
■ waiting for work to be scheduled;
■ waiting for materials or tools;
■ waiting for instructions.

Idle time is not normally charged directly against the job, but is regarded as a production overhead, or overhead incurred in providing a service. But if the fault can be traced to one particular department, it may be charged against that department.

For instance, say a factory maintenance programme, scheduled to be completed over a weekend shutdown runs late and production time is lost once everybody is back at work.

It seems obvious that in this case the fault can be traced back to the maintenance department and the cost of the idle time will be charged to it. In that case all the managers in the maintenance department have got some explaining to do.

4.3 Cost centres and overheads

Some overheads belong entirely to one cost centre, while some can be shared among several cost centres.

Where an overhead can belong entirely to one cost centre we say that it is **allocated** to the appropriate cost centre. The first line manager of that cost centre will bear the responsibility for controlling these overhead costs within the cost centre.

Activity 30

3 mins

Think of two overhead costs from your own workplace which could be allocated entirely to one cost centre.

_____

_____

It's unlikely that we've thought of the same things, but here are a couple of examples that spring to mind:

■ the wages of a manager in the food hall of a large superstore will be allocated to the food hall cost centre;
■ the cost of an advertising promotion will be allocated to the marketing cost centre.

Activity 31

3 mins

Here are some more overhead costs, which are similar in that they can be allocated entirely to individual cost centres. Against each one, write down which of the following three classes of overheads it belongs to: production overheads, administration overheads or selling and distribution overheads.

■ Wages of managers working entirely within a particular production department.

_____

■ Paint, oil and grease used in a certain production department.

_____

■ Wages of receptionists.

_____

■ Travelling expenses of sales staff.

_____

The first two costs are production overheads, the wages of receptionists are likely to be an administrative overhead and the travelling expenses of the sales staff are a selling overhead. Each of these could be allocated directly and entirely to one cost centre, and the responsibility of controlling them is that of the cost centre manager.

Often, though, overhead costs have to be spread over a number of cost centres. These costs are controlled first of all in one cost centre and then **apportioned** between other cost centres, using an agreed method of deciding how they should be shared out or apportioned.

Here are some overhead costs that might be apportioned among various departments. I've also shown the cost centre where the cost would initially be controlled, and suggested a possible method for apportioning the cost between all departments.

Type of cost	Cost centre where cost is initially controlled	Possible method of apportionment
Rent and rates	Property manager	Floor area occupied by various departments
Lighting and heating	Plant engineer	Building volume occupied by various departments
Insurance of equipment	Administration manager	Value of equipment in various departments

Activity 32 ·

5 mins

In the space provided below, write down which cost centre you think should initially control each overhead and suggest a method by which they could fairly be apportioned.

Type of cost	Cost centre where cost is initially controlled	Possible method of apportionment
Staff welfare Advertising for staff Building repairs		

Here are my suggestions. You may have thought of other equally reasonable suggestions, so don't feel that our answers have to be the same.

> Where possible it is preferable to **allocate** overheads directly to cost centres, if there are clear and agreed bases for doing so rather than to **apportion** them between cost centres, as the overheads are identified as being generated by, or the responsibility of, those cost centres.

Type of cost	Cost centre where cost is initially controlled	Possible method of apportionment
Staff welfare	Personnel manager	Number of staff per department
Advertising for staff	Personnel manager	Number of vacancies notified per department
Building repairs	Building and works manager	Floor area per department

There is no hard-and-fast method of apportioning overheads. But methods should be logical.

How much control can first line managers have over costs that have been apportioned to them, rather than allocated to them directly?

The answer is somewhere between very little and none.

Looking at the example above, you should be able to see that the first line manager of a department cannot control at all how much the personnel manager spends on staff welfare. Whether they are charged at all for advertising staff vacancies can be controlled to some extent by limiting the number of staff being recruited. But how much per vacancy the personnel department spends is beyond their control.

How far can a departmental first line manager control the costs apportioned to the department for building repairs?

_____

_____

_____

How much money the Building and Works Manager spends is beyond the first line manager's control, as is (in the short term) the chargeable floor area occupied by the department. The only way the first line manager can exercise some control is in trying to ensure that the department doesn't cause building repairs to be necessary.

It is not necessary for you to know more about the accounting process of allocating, approving or transferring costs. It is this awareness of costs, not accounting manipulations, which is the key to success. Cost consciousness is important managerial behaviour. Apart from being aware of information on costs how is a cost-conscious attitude fostered?

5 Cost consciousness

We've seen that controlling and keeping down costs demands continued effort. You have to be permanently on the look-out for performance levels falling, materials and equipment being wrongly used, bottlenecks, idle time, untidy and slipshod ways of working and so on.

Clearly you can only do so much yourself. You need the support of the workteam in looking for and maintaining ways of keeping down costs, and in keeping records of what is actually happening in your work areas.

If one person tries to keep costs down on their own by turning off lights when they go out, it will have little effect. But if that person can persuade a dozen others to do the same, increasing amounts can be saved.

So what can we do to make the workteam aware of the costs and become enthusiastic about keeping them down?

Activity 34

4 mins

S/NVQ B1.2

This Activity may provide the basis of evidence for your S/NVQ portfolio. If you are intending to take this course of action, it might be better to write your answers on separate sheets of paper.

Suggest two ways in which you think you could make your workteam more cost conscious. How would you implement your suggestions?

_____

_____

_____

_____

Typical answers might include:

- getting the workteam more involved;
- encouraging them to make suggestions;
- offering prizes for suggestions on how to keep costs down;
- passing on information about costs;
- telling them when costs increase or decrease.

Perhaps you might talk to your workteam or put up notices and then follow up with meetings, discussions and so on.

If you are compiling an S/NVQ portfolio you may be able to use notices and testimony from your workteam members and your manager as the basis of possible acceptable evidence.

5.1 Spotting the need for cost consciousness and control

To be really successful at being conscious of costs and hence controlling them, you have to be aware of those areas of your workteam's operations where costs may be a problem. One way to do this is by analysing costs in terms of variances. As we have seen, these show both the cause of the cost and its size. Together the analysis allows us to both spot a problem and do something about it.

Activity 35

Look at the possible adverse variances below. Against each one, jot down what you could do to affect them.

Materials

Adverse price variance

_____

Adverse usage variance

_____

Labour

Adverse efficiency variance

_____

Adverse rate variance

_____

Adverse idle time variance

_____

Overheads

Adverse price variance

_____

You will probably have jotted down answers based on what is familiar to you, but in general I expect our answers will not be very different from each other.

Materials price variance	Check that the best price possible is being obtained for materials from suppliers
Materials usage variance	Check that there is not excessive wastage in the process
Labour efficiency variance	Check that staff are working effectively and have all the equipment and training that they need to do so

Labour rate variance	Check that staff of the right grade are being used on appropriate work, and that unnecessary overtime is not being worked
Labour idle time variance	Check that work is flowing smoothly into the workteam, and that there are no holdups such as for machine breakdowns
Overhead variance	Check that the workteam is not incurring unnecessary overheads and that prices obtained are reasonable.

One other factor to bear in mind: it is always possible that the standard against which variances are measured has become out of date. This means that it is not your control of costs that is in question, but the relevance of the variances in the first place.

The three keys to success in raising cost-consciousness are:

- **involvement;**

- **communication;**

- **feedback.**

5.2 Involvement and communication

Cost consciousness means treating costs in the workplace as though *your* money was going to be used to pay for them. Successfully finding ways of keeping costs down means keeping an eye on your spending all the time, rather than looking for one good idea. In the end your job and the money you earn depend on a successful operation, of which controlling costs is an important element.

We need to communicate with people about cost if we want them to become involved. The trouble is, much of the information used in the workplace to monitor costs is likely to be in the form of financial statements that are not easy to understand and which can easily put people off.

You and other team leaders need to give your team members information about costs in terms that are relevant, timely and in an appropriate place.

Activity 36

3 mins

Here are two ways of communicating information about a quarterly electricity bill.

Tick whichever you think would make you more conscious of the cost of the electricity you are using.

a ☐

> NOTICE
>
> The electricity bill for the last quarter was:
>
> £2321.41
>
> *Save it!*

b ☐

> The cost per copy of using this photocopier is 6p
>
> Don't make more copies than you need!

We can make a case for saying that either of these would be effective for different people. Let's look at (a) first.

Sometimes the sheer size of a sum of money, like the cost of this electricity bill, can give people a jolt. £2321.41 sounds a lot more serious than 6p per photocopied sheet.

However, large figures quickly baffle us and tend not to mean a lot. Electricity bills of £1500, £2400 or £13,967 all sound equally terrifying if our quarterly bill at home is about £100.

It's all too easy to feel that such a large sum is nothing to do with us. We feel that we didn't contribute much to the bill in the first place and there is nothing we can do to reduce it.

Knowing that each photocopy we take costs 6p is likely to make a bigger impression, because it relates directly to what we are doing, particularly if we have to use a counter that charges copies directly to our budget.

So, I would say that (b) is more likely to raise peoples awareness of the costs and prompt them to try to do something about them than (a).

This sort of information doesn't just have to be in the form of some kind of notice. Just saying something like:

> 'This aluminium wrapper is £50 a roll now. I don't think we should let it get knocked about.'

or

> 'We've just spent £200 having these blades reset. Better make sure that no grit gets in there.'

may have a similar effect.

Activity 37

Refer back to the two notices about costs.

Which do you think is a more effective place to display the information these notices contain: on the canteen notice-board or above the photocopier?

_____

Information about costs will make more impact if it is provided where the cost is about to be incurred and just as it's going to be incurred.

What we read as we are about to use a piece of equipment is harder to avoid than information on the canteen notice-board.

Of course, like many notices, we can get used to them in time and fail to see them. It is useful to replace them with new and different, but striking, notices regularly.

We can say that information about costs needs to be:

- in a form we can relate to;
- at the time and place the cost is incurred.

5.3 Feedback

Now let's look at feedback – the response you give to the workteam's efforts to keep costs down or to their suggestions for cost savings.

Activity 38 · 3 mins

Suppose somebody in your workplace suggests a change to a certain process that will reduce costs. The change is approved and made, and there is an article about it in the house newspaper. Write down two important pieces of information that you would hope to find in the article.

_____

_____

You may have had several ideas but I hope among them would be:

- the name of the person who made the suggestion;
- how much money it will save.

If we are to be aware of costs, we want to know how much we're saving by our efforts. Certainly, if we're going to maintain an interest in costs, we need to know that we're making progress. By recognizing who suggested the cost saving, further emphasis is placed on its importance.

Of course, not all suggestions are necessarily good ideas.

Activity 39 · 2 mins

Somebody in your workteam suggests changing your computer stationery supplier. He has spoken to a representative from an alternative supplier and obtained some prices. On the face of it, it looks as though the alternative supplier's prices are less than you are currently paying. Investigating further, you find that the prices apply only to larger volume purchases than you would make and that the existing supplier has a better reputation for quality and reliability.

Tick the appropriate box to indicate if you would:

a let the subject drop because telling your workteam member might discourage him from making further suggestions ☐

b tell him that it wasn't a workable idea ☐

c thank him for taking the trouble to find out about the alternative supplier and explain why you weren't going to take up the suggestion ☐

You probably chose (c).

EXTENSION 3
Chapter 7 of
David Doyle's book *Cost Control: A Strategic Guide* looks at cost responsibility and awareness in some depth.

It is easy to understand that, even though the suggestion isn't taken up, people need feedback on their ideas if they are to maintain an interest. However, it's not easy to remember to supply that feedback when we're under a lot of pressure to do all sorts of other jobs.

It's worth making the effort, however. If you don't encourage cost consciousness, even when it is not directly useful, it won't be there when you need it.

6 Checklists for controlling costs

Finding ways of controlling costs and keeping them down depends upon thinking about every situation in the workplace and asking whether we are making the best possible use of the resources involved and doing the task in question in the most efficient way.

The questions we need to ask ourselves, and the answers we will get, will vary with the job and the workplace.

I hope you will find the following checklists help you to channel your thoughts as you examine your work area to ensure you have your workteam operating efficiently. Use the space provided to make your own notes.

6.1 Checklist for the workteam

■ Do I use people with the right amount of skill for the job in hand?

_____

■ Do I use highly paid people for low level work? If so, why? Can it be avoided?

_____

_____

■ Are salaries reviewed regularly?

_____

■ Is all our overtime necessary?

_____

■ What causes idle time?

- ■ Lack of materials? ☐ _____

- ■ Lack of available equipment? ☐ _____

- ■ Lack of precise instructions? ☐ _____

- ■ Lack of supervision? ☐ _____

■ Is the workteam good about timekeeping?

_____

■ Are all the members of the workteam fully trained?

_____

■ Is the workteam fully competent?

_____

■ Do their skills need bringing up to date?

_____

■ Is career development taken seriously?

_____

■ Are they willing to try new ideas?

_____

■ Is there any information they would like to know about the workplace, the organization or the product?

_____

■ How often do I make a point of chatting to them about themselves and the job?

_____

■ Do I ever have to explain what I want done several times?

_____

■ Should I write instructions for any tasks the workteam do?

_____

■ Are written instructions up to date, in the right place and readable?

_____

■ Do I give the workteam feedback on their performance regularly (not just when things go wrong)?

_____

■ What is our absenteeism record like?

_____

■ How many of the workteam have left in the past two years? Why?

_____

■ Have the workteam any special skills or knowledge which we're not using?

_____

■ What records do I keep to help make the best possible use of the workteam?

_____

6.2 Checklist for materials

■ Do we use the cheapest materials for the purpose without reducing the quality?

_____

■ Do we run out of materials? Why?

_____

■ Do we have any out-of-date materials? Why?

_____

■ Are any materials damaged during storage?

_____

■ What control have I over:

  ■ production materials?

  ■ consumables – bags, stationery, paper, oil, grease, packing materials, cleaning materials, etc.?

_____

_____

■ Is scrap or waste material increasing/decreasing? Is work having to be done again to reach appropriate standards? Why?

_____

■ Is the workplace clean and tidy? How often do I check housekeeping?

_____

6.3 Checklist for overheads

■ Do I report equipment faults as soon as they occur?

_____

■ Do I keep a record of the date and reason for machine failure?

_____

■ Is all our equipment regularly maintained?

_____

■ How fully used is the equipment for which I am responsible?

_____

■ Could we get rid of any out-of-date machines?

_____

■ Can I improve the layout of the equipment in my work area?

_____

■ Are any machines standing idle? Why?

_____

■ Do we switch off lights and power when they are not needed?

_____

■ Do we backup overnight whenever possible? Do we reroute calls through a cheaper call provider, or use e-mail?

_____

■ What changes would I like to introduce in the way we work which will make us more efficient?

_____

■ Which departments do I need to help me to do this?

_____

_____

_____

7 Cost reduction

So far we have looked at controlling costs within a situation where the same level of operations is being carried out. But there are times when an organization has to make difficult decisions about what it is doing, how and where. A business may be losing money, or a non-profit organization may have lost funding. There may be no choice but to 'cut costs' by:

■ closing down parts of its operations;
■ ceasing to make an unprofitable product or to provide a service that is not cost-effective;
■ outsourcing a service that is currently provided in-house, so that it is provided more economically by someone outside the organization.

Although these decisions will be made by senior managers, as a first line manager you may become caught up in this cost reduction process.

More than ever, it is important in this case to:

■ have information (on what costs need reducing and how and when this will be done);
■ communicate with your workteam (to provide information and feedback and to involve them).

In some ways cost reduction can be said to be a more extreme form of cost control; but as it usually involves a cutback in the scale of operations it is a more difficult and painful process, often leading to redundancies, and the sale of buildings and machinery.

Activity 40 · 5 mins

The School Meals Service has informed all school meals managers that their individual meals service must break even or be closed down and replaced by private contractors.

Isabel Smith, a school meals manager, can produce and sell a maximum of 1,000 meals per week.

She is told her weekly fixed overheads are £2,000. Education authority policy is to charge £1·50 per meal and Isabel cannot alter this.

She calculates that the variable costs per meal, all raw materials, are £0·50.

Work out the break-even for Isabel's canteen.

$$\frac{\text{Fixed overheads}}{\text{Contribution}} = \underline{\hspace{2cm}} = \underline{\hspace{2cm}} \text{ meals}$$

We can see that Isabel's position is fairly desperate! Here are her break-even calculations.

$$\frac{£2,000}{£1·00} = 2,000 \text{ meals.}$$

She cannot produce 2,000 meals because her limit for production and sales is 1,000. Unless she is allowed to increase prices drastically, close-down seems inevitable.

If she could raise her prices to £2·50, her surplus would be £2·00 per meal and, if she could sell her maximum number of meals (1,000), she would just break even.

Activity 41

S/NVQs B1.1, *or* B1.2

This Activity may provide the basis of appropriate evidence for your S/NVQ portfolio. If you are intending to take this course of action, it might be better to write your answers on separate sheets of paper.

Have you been faced with such a problem as described above, requiring you to control your resources or make recommendations for the use of your resources so that costs can be cut?

Write down the tasks you had to complete and the reasons you were given for the changes needed.

_____

_____

_____

_____

_____

_____

Your response will be related to your own job. Perhaps you had to contribute to a decision whether a member of your workteam should be made redundant or to think about whether a new piece of equipment would prove cheaper than one or two new people in the long term.

Self-assessment 3

10 mins

1 a Name the two types of cost included in prime cost.

_____

_____

  b What additional costs are added to prime cost to arrive at the total factory cost?

_____

2 State what is meant by a cost centre.

_____

3 Identify the three characteristics of a good cost system.

_____

_____

_____

4 State the three keys to success in making a workteam more cost conscious.

_____

_____

_____

5 How would you ensure that a worker's attention was drawn to information about costs?

_____

_____

_____

6 Why is it useful to use a checklist when examining your work area for ways to decrease costs?

_____

_____

Answers to these questions can be found on page 101.

8 Summary

- Managers need cost information to make decisions.

- Direct costs are related to the individual unit produced, e.g. cost of raw materials.

- Overhead costs cannot be directly attributed to any one unit of production or service provided.

- Cost units are identifiable items against which the costs of a company, department or other defined part of the organization can be related.

- Cost centres are locations where costs can be conveniently collected and grouped.

- A cost coding system can be used for tracking every cost in the workplace.

- Direct material and labour costs are collected in cost centres and charged directly to the job. Overheads are also applied to job costs; many are estimates.

- To make the workteam cost conscious:
  - involve them;
  - pass on information;
  - give them feedback.

- Information about costs needs to be:
  - in simple terms which we can relate to;
  - available where and when the costs are incurred.

Session D
Preparing a budget

1 Introduction

In Session B we saw that standard costing tells us what a product should cost to make, or what a service should cost to provide. We know how important and useful information is in raising cost consciousness, and in allowing us to pinpoint – by means of variances – areas for immediate cost control action.

We also saw that standard costs can become out of date, so that what looks like a cause for concern is actually just a natural development over time.

All this implies that information must be gathered and fed into the system so that costs can be monitored against it. And at some point it must be updated so that costs can be monitored against revised figures.

In this session we shall look briefly first at the nature of a budget, and then at how first line managers can be involved in gathering information for both formulating the original budget, and updating it over time.

2 What is a budget?

As the manager of your workteam you are probably fully aware of what you need to get done, and by when. You also know how many team members you are responsible for, what they can do and what they need to allow them to do it. In other words, you have a plan, and you must answer to your own manager for achieving that plan.

The place where this plan is set down in monetary terms is called the budget. A budget can be described as:

'a quantitative plan of action prepared in advance of a defined period of time'.

For more material on budgets, refer to the Super Series workbook *Budgeting for Better Performance*.

Activity 42

Janice Dyer's team provides user support for a software business. She has a team of four people, each of whom is paid £500 per week, and she is paid £700 per week. The workteam uses equipment which costs £1,000 per week to run, and uses materials that cost £200 per week. What is Janice's total budgeted expenditure for one week?

I hope you can see that Janice's total budget is £2,000 for team members, £700 for herself, £1,000 for equipment, and £200 for materials – a total of £3,900.

It would be easy to use this analysis of Janice's costs to calculate a break-even point.

Activity 43

Assume that each user seeking software support pays a minimum of £10.00 per call to Janice's team. How many calls per week would the team have to answer to cover their costs?

Again you should have found this quite straightforward: the break-even number of calls is simply £3,900/£10 = 390 calls.

The budget therefore gives Janice a very clear plan of action for the period ahead.

If you work in an organization whose main purpose is to provide a service (a hospital or a library, for instance), you are likely to look at things differently.

Budgets are prepared in a slightly different way in organizations that set out to make a profit, compared with those that don't. We'll look at the way different organizations go about obtaining information for budgets and putting them together.

3 Gathering and co-ordinating information

3.1 Preparation of sales estimates

In most organizations the **key** or **limiting** factor has to be worked out first, as it is the factor on which all other budgets depend. In profit-seeking businesses the limiting factor is usually sales. This means that the business has a limited ability to expand sales beyond a certain level and so must assume that it can only achieve that level.

The sales department forecast has to be made before colleagues in purchasing or production can make theirs. There is no point in production planning to produce 10,000 items, if only 5,000 can be sold. But different functions of the business have to work closely to prepare budgets. It's no use sales planning to sell far more than production can produce either.

The person who prepares the sales budget has a special responsibility: to determine the sales forecast for the coming year as accurately as possible. If this is wrong, everybody else's budget will be wrong too.

Information for sales forecast can be gathered by internal and external methods:

■ **Internal methods**

- Reports from sales representatives.
- Statistical analysis of past sales records to identify trends that seem likely to continue.

■ **External methods**

- Market research information about customers' likes and dislikes and about what competitors are doing.
- Information about the general economic climate, which may tell you whether people are likely to be spending more or less money on, say, sweets and chocolates.

Using **internal methods** entails finding out information from within the company's own records, maybe just by summing up individual sales representatives' forecasts.

Using **external methods** involves going outside the business. You may use your own staff to research some of this information, and you may glean some from official publications.

Activity 44 · 5 mins

Suggest **one** possible benefit of internal methods and **one** possible disadvantage.

_____

_____

_____

_____

There is not necessarily one right answer to this Activity but the following springs to mind.

- One major benefit of internal methods is that they involve a lot of people at all levels in the budget process. Provided they understand what they're doing and why, and realize how important it is, they can make people feel more interested in and committed to the company and the job.
- The major disadvantage of internal methods is that they only reflect what is happening inside the business. They don't take into account changes in economic conditions, or what the competition is doing. Estimates produced by internal methods only may tend to be over-optimistic.

A good sales forecast may be based on an **internal** forecast, which is adjusted at a senior level to take account of available **external** data.

3.2 The budget

Once the important estimates, particularly sales, have been made, other things start to fall into place. The rest of the budget, described in money terms, can then be produced.

We've already worked out that, once the sales estimate is known, it's possible to produce the production budget. What comes next?

Activity 45

3 mins

Below is a diagram of the budgets prepared so far. Below is a list of some of the remaining budgets that still have to be prepared. Fill in the budget you think should follow next in the preparation sequence from the list of budgets still to be prepared:

- departmental expense budget;
- cash budget;
- resources budget.

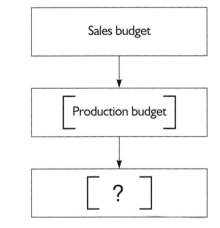

Sequence of budgets

Once you've prepared the production budget and decided what production levels are planned in the coming year, given forecast sales, you will have to plan the resources you need to meet these levels. Thus, the resources budget comes next in the sequence. In practice, this involves preparing three separate budgets for the following production costs.

- **Material usage:** required quantities and costs of all materials needed to meet planned production levels.
- **Labour:** the number of person hours needed to meet production targets, and the cost of those hours.
- **Equipment use:** the operating hours required on each piece of equipment or group of machines, and the cost of those hours.

If you work in a manufacturing industry, this may well be very much your territory. As a first line manager, you probably have a key role in this area of resource planning and control.

Activity 46

Identify **two** consequences of poor supervision in each of the three main resource budget areas.

Material usage

_____

_____

Labour

_____

_____

Equipment use

_____

_____

There may be a wide range of consequences. Certainly poor supervision may lead to overspending. Here are just some of the consequences you may have noted.

■ Poor supervision of **material usage** could lead to:

- more scrap;
- pilferage;
- bottle-necks in production or idle time.

■ Poor supervision of **labour** could lead to:

- low quality work or more scrap;
- poor timekeeping;
- increased overtime budget.

■ Poor supervision of **equipment use** could lead to:

- more breakdowns;
- more idle time;
- higher maintenance costs;
- more scrap.

Now let's see how preparing the resources budget leads to the next budget in the sequence by working through an example.

Activity 47

4 mins

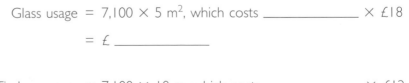

Unique Windows Ltd manufacture double-glazed windows for which the basic materials are timber and glass.

Budget sales for the coming year are 7,100 units. Unique has no stock of materials or finished windows at the end of the year.

A standard window uses:

■ 5 m² glass, which costs £18 per square metre;
■ 10 m timber, which costs £12 per metre.

What will be the total materials usage to meet the required production of 7,100 standard windows?

Glass usage $= 7{,}100 \times 5$ m², which costs _____ $\times$ £18

$= £$ _____

Timber usage $= 7{,}100 \times 10$ m, which costs _____ $\times$ £12

$= £$ _____

In order to produce 7,100 units the materials usage would be:

Glass usage = 7,100 × 5 m², which costs 35,500 × £18 = £639,000;

Timber usage = 7,100 × 10 m, which costs 71,000 × £12 = £852,000.

Now we know how much material usage is planned we know how much will have to be bought in.

One thing you must not forget when providing information for budget preparation is to take account of materials that have already been purchased. How would the purchases budget be affected if the organization already has some materials in stock at the beginning of the year?

Activity 48 · 3 mins

Ramesh Said has been told to produce 6,000 units of production in June. Each unit of production requires 5 kg of Material A. At the beginning of June there are 4,500 kg of Material A in stock, and at the end of June there needs to be 7,000 kg of Material A to cope with a big order at the beginning of July.

How much Material A must Ramesh plan to purchase in June? Fill in the spaces below.

Material A		*kg*
To be used in June	(6,000 × 5)	30,000
Add: needed in stock 30 June		
Deduct: Held in stock 1 June		————
Equals: Purchases in June		————

I hope you can see that the amount planned to be held in stock at the end of the period has to be added to the usage in the period to arrive at the total amount required, but that only this figure LESS the amount held in stock at the beginning of the period has to be bought.

Material A		*kg*
To be used in June	(6,000 × 5)	30,000
Add: needed in stock 30 June		7,000
		37,000
Deduct: Held in stock 1 June		(4,500)
Equals: Purchases in June		32,500

But don't forget that the resources budget must also contain the plan for the use of machines and labour, as well as the materials needed, to meet planned production levels. So calculations like the one we have just been looking at will also have to be carried out for machine use and labour.

We said earlier that budget preparation is different in some respects if you are not in the business of manufacturing something. So let's now have a look at the parallel stages of budget preparation in organizations that offer some kind of service.

4 Service industries and the public sector

A service industry may provide transport, for instance, or supply gas or electricity, or it may offer medical services. There are many thousands of service organizations which we all depend on.

Private service industries have to make a profit in order to stay in business; an example is a haulage contractor that transports goods manufactured by other businesses. Some public organizations (NHS hospitals, for instance) do not expect to make a profit, but have to plan to provide the best service they can with the money they are allocated. This means that the budgeting process in the public sector is more or less identical to the approach in the private sector.

Let's look first at the budget development for Tim Hawkins, haulage contractor.

Activity 49 · 2 mins

Tim starts at the same point as a manufacturer – estimating sales in the coming period. In his case, the sales will be the number of contracts to carry goods that Tim thinks he can win.

Having determined the sales budget, what do you think will be the next stage in budget preparation for Tim Hawkins' business?

_____

_____

I hope you decided that the next stage was to plan the resources required to meet planned sales: how many lorries, how many drivers, etc.

So Tim's budget sequence might look something like this.

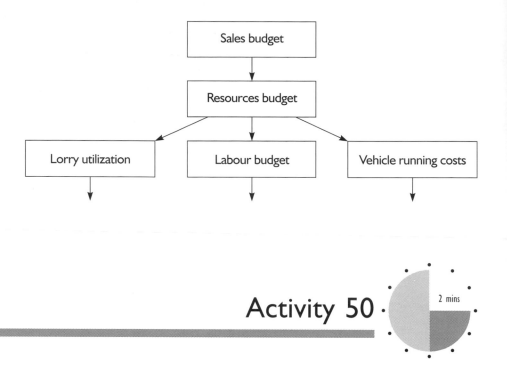

Activity 50

2 mins

What might Tim Hawkins do if his present resources were insufficient to meet budgeted sales? Write down **two** suggestions.

_____

_____

He could do a number of things including:

■ purchasing or hiring more lorries;
■ using his existing fleet of lorries and drivers more efficiently;
■ refusing the contracts that he couldn't meet with his present resources.

If he had more resources than he needed to meet budgeted sales, on the other hand, he might decide to:

■ lay off staff;
■ dispose of surplus lorries;
■ reduce his prices to attract business.

Any or all of these decisions would have to be tackled at his next stage of budget preparation.

National Health Service trusts and hospitals, too, are clearly concerned with making the best use of available resources, but in their case the limiting factor is not usually their equivalent of 'sales', i.e. the demand for beds from sick patients. It is instead the allocation of resources, which the hospitals receive from central government.

Hospitals rarely find they have too many resources available, as the demand for health care grows continually. Hospitals do make cuts in their budgets, but this is usually due to a cut in the reduced basic availability of resources and funds, rather than because demand is reduced.

In a hospital, the number of beds can be used as a limiting factor. An estimate can be made as to the occupancy or utilization of each bed through the year. This is similar to the way in which hotels budget, although basic cost information about the length of stay of a variety of patients is more complex than business or holiday visitors to a hotel. A private hospital will budget on bed occupancy and the price paid for bed use against the costs of providing care.

5 Departmental budgets

What happens inside organizations, so far as budgeting is concerned? Although there will be some variation in details, departmental budget preparation is similar in most types of organization.

At the same time as the sales and production budgets are being produced, managers and supervisors in every department are having to estimate how much it will cost them to carry out their responsibilities in the coming period.

Many of us provide a sort of back-up service to the main function of the business we're in. Thus, if a firm makes furniture, the job of departments such as sales, finance, the administration office, the computer section, design, materials testing and so on, can all be regarded as providing back-up services to the manufacturing process. We can even argue that the factory itself provides a back-up service, since it is not directly part of the manufacturing process. We have seen that these back-up costs are known as **overheads**. Sometimes deciding what is, and what is not, an overhead can be quite difficult. Nevertheless, it is very important for any organization to identify overheads and to keep them under control.

To give you an Idea of what's involved in preparing departmental budgets in order that a full picture of overheads can be built up, let's look at some examples.

Activity 51 ·

In the Nottinghamshire factory, all lorries delivering materials or taking away finished goods have to get security clearance before coming up to the loading bay of the stores. The factory runs 24 hours a day, so routine maintenance and factory cleaning has to take place while production is running. This results in as little disruption to the schedule as possible.

This description of activities in a factory contains clues to some of the departmental budgets which will have to be prepared. Suggest **three** of them, and say who you think might be responsible for preparing them.

The information should have made it possible for you to pick out the likely budgets. The titles of the people responsible for preparing different budgets may vary. The overall responsibility would lie with the factory manager.

- Maintenance budget: responsibility of the maintenance engineer.
- Stores budget: responsibility of the stores controller.
- Cleaning budget: responsibility of the domestic services manager.
- Security budget: responsibility of the chief security officer.

Each of these areas will make an important contribution to production, even though it isn't directly part of the production process.

We could repeat this exercise for other functions in any organization. In sales, for example, there may well be:

- an advertising and sales promotion budget;
- a sales staff budget;
- a van fleet maintenance budget; and so on.

In the preparation of an administration budget, there would be budgets for the accounts section, the computer section, secretarial services and personnel services.

You can probably break down any major function in your own workplace in the same way. You can therefore see that the preparation of a departmental budget needs an enormous amount of information and planning from a large number of people.

Although the most senior person in any one function will have overall responsibility for the departmental budget, you or your manager may well have a large degree of responsibility for the budget in your particular area.

Once you start to examine costs in your area, you will find that, as in every other area in your workplace, there are both:

■ fixed costs, and
■ variable costs: the cost that varies with the level of activity.

How are variable costs incorporated into a budget process, given that the actual level of activity, which will 'fix' these costs, is not known?

Here's an example of the sort of forecast a sales manager might produce to deal with variable costs.

	Pessimistic sales forecast	Expected sales	Optimistic sales forecast
	£3,000,000	£4,000,000	£5,000,000
Overheads	£	£	£
Commission (2%)	60,000	80,000	100,000
Distribution costs (5%)	150,000	200,000	250,000
Variable costs	210,000	280,000	350,000
Basic salaries (sales staff)	90,000	90,000	90,000
Manager's salary	30,000	30,000	30,000
Sales office costs	20,000	20,000	20,000
Fixed costs	140,000	140,000	140,000
Total overheads	350,000	420,000	490,000
% of sales	11.67%	10.5%	9.8%

Variable costs rise or fall as sales rise. We can see from the forecast above that all distribution costs and all commissions rise as sales rise. These are variable costs; the other costs remain fixed.

Activity 52 ·

4 mins

Look at the sales manager's forecast. Make a note of what happens to overheads as a percentage of sales if the expected level of sales rises.

_____

_____

_____

_____

Because some of the costs are fixed the overheads, shown as a percentage of sales, decline as anticipated sales increase.

It's easy to regard fixed costs as something of a millstone round your neck, particularly if it is difficult to make sales. But, as we see from this example, if business is booming they decrease as a percentage of the total business activity and become less of a worry.

Self-assessment 4

15 mins

1   Complete the following by filling in the missing words.

The _____ or _____ factor is the factor on which all other budgets depend.

2   Armot Ltd produces 12,000 tables each year, but in the next year sales should increase by 10 per cent. Stock levels of tables should reduce from 2000 to 1320 units.

Calculate the planned production level for the forthcoming year.

_____

_____

_____

3   Identify whether the following represent internal or external sources of information for budgeting for a school.

	Internal	External
a Details of birth rates and newly built local housing.	☐	☐
b Advice from teachers about new books and equipment needs.	☐	☐
c National pay awards for teachers.	☐	☐

4   Identify whether poor supervision of equipment use, materials usage or labour lead to each of the following effects.

Effects/Poor supervision of	Equipment use	Materials usage	Labour
poor timekeeping	☐	☐	☐
breakdowns	☐	☐	☐
pilferage	☐	☐	☐

5   State briefly why organizations maintain departmental budgets.

_____

_____

Answers to these questions can be found on pages 101–2.

6 Summary

- Estimating sales based on the reports of sales staff and/or external conditions will usually be the starting point of the budget process in organizations that sell goods or services.

- Knowing the allocation of funds is often the starting point in non-profit organizations.

- Production levels and costs can be determined once sales are estimated.

- The share of expenses (overheads) allocated to departments will be estimated once sales and production levels have been forecast.

- Some expenses will be fixed and some variable. Higher levels of business activity reduce the impact of fixed costs as they are spread over more units.

- Your main role as a first line manager in the budget process will probably be in providing information for the budget forecast and resource planning and control, and in providing updated information if the budget is to be revised.

Performance checks

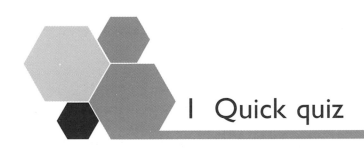

1 Quick quiz

Write down your answers in the spaces below to the following questions on *Controlling Costs.*

Question 1   Complete the equation: Sales – Costs = _____

Question 2   What is meant by fixed costs?

_____

Question 3   How would you define the wages of security staff in cost terms?

_____

Question 4   Why cannot a first line manager always control costs?

_____

Question 5   Name two types of standard.

_____

Question 6   Why are variances analysed?

_____

Question 7   What is indicated by an adverse efficiency variance?

_____

Question 8   Name the two elements of standard cost.

_____

Question 9   What is a cost centre?

_____

Question 10   Briefly explain how a cost code is used.

_____

_____

_____

Question 11   Briefly explain what is meant by idle time.

_____

Question 12   Why is it important to get the workteam fully involved in controlling costs?

_____

_____

Question 13   How can you maintain the interest of your workteam in controlling costs?

_____

_____

Question 14   What is the significance of a limiting factor in the budget process?

_____

_____

Answers to these questions can be found on page 103.

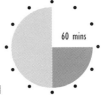

2 Workbook assessment

Read the following case incident and then deal with the questions which follow, writing your answers on a separate sheet of paper.

Pat is the catering supervisor of an organization which has decided to provide lunch for its 300 employees.

Senior managers have estimated that 80 per cent of their employees will use the restaurant for a meal on five days a week for 50 weeks in a year.

The menu, with limited choice, will be offered at a self-service counter.

An average meal is not to exceed £1.20 in materials cost to the restaurant.

The following estimates have been made.

■ Gas, electricity and heating: £10,000.
■ Crockery, cutlery and replacements: £2,000.
■ Cleaning, laundry and sundries: £3,000.

Pat, as catering supervisor, is paid £18,000 a year.

Wages for kitchen and other staff are £5,000 a month for 12 months in a year.

1   How many meals will Pat need to provide daily?

2   What is your estimate for the number of meals per year?

3   Identify and quantify the following costs for a cost statement.

   a Labour costs.
   b Material costs.
   c Overheads.

d Total sales required to cover the costs.

e The average selling price per meal needed to cover costs.

4 If the organization decides to charge £2 for a three-course lunch, how much is it going to have to subsidize each meal?

5 What percentage will this organizational subsidy be of the annual sales through the restaurant?

6 As catering supervisor Pat has many areas of the restaurant and kitchen to control. What are they? Explain as fully as you can what Pat will need to control and how.

3 Work-based assignment

S/NVQ B1.1, B1.2

The time guide for this assignment gives you an approximate idea of how long it is likely to take you to write up your findings. You will need to spend some additional time gathering information, perhaps talking to colleagues and thinking about the assignment. As you research and report, you should aim to develop your personal competency too in focusing clearly on results and influencing others with the aim of improving cost control. Ensure that you talk to people at mutually acceptable times so that the information you receive is of the best quality and that people are fully committed to helping you. You may need to convince them of the value of your work, for instance.

This Activity may provide the basis of evidence for your S/NVQ portfolio. If you are intending to take this course of action, it might be better to write your answers on separate sheets of paper.

There may be some form of cost control in your workplace. The following questions ask you to find out something about it and your role in the cost control system.

Take any product or service which your workplace is involved with and discover the following.

1 The cost of the product or service. If it is a service, explain the cost in the form of an appropriate cost unit.

2 The prime cost of the product – this is all the direct costs.

3   The overheads content of the product/service cost broken down into:

    a factory or production overheads;
    b administrative overheads;
    c selling and distribution overheads.

4   The cost centre that you are connected to and the total cost of that cost centre for the year broken down, where appropriate, into departments and overheads.

5   The way in which the importance of cost control is communicated and how the workforce is motivated towards cost awareness. What is your role in this?

If this is not possible, use the checklists for keeping costs down to provide data for a report to your manager or trainer.

Prepare a report entitled 'Improving our control over costs' after analysing the effectiveness and relevance of present systems. Make appropriate recommendations for improvements and discuss your findings with your manager or trainer.

Reflect and review

1 Reflect and review

Now that you'll have completed your work on *Controlling Costs*, let's review our workbook objectives.

You should be better able to:

■ identify different costs and how they behave.

You have looked at direct and indirect costs, and materials, labour and general overhead costs.

■ Which types of cost are under your control? What flexibility do you have in controlling them?

_____

_____

_____

_____

Costs can be classified in order to analyse them in the workplace. This allows us to record and control costs. We have worked through costing and in doing so seen how costs occur. Everything that happens within the workplace leads to a cost in some way.

■ As a first line manager, can you clearly identify the main areas of cost in your work area and are you aware of the types of cost? Do any areas need clarifying? Make notes of any points which come to mind below.

_____

_____

_____

_____

■ Is your role in controlling costs clear, bearing in mind some areas of cost may need clarification? Are you fully in control of costs which are your responsibility? Are clarifications or changes needed?

_____

_____

_____

■ appreciate how important it is to control costs.

Fixed and variable costs are also important in organizations. It is unlikely that you can do much about fixed costs, but you can make best use of resources under your control which may be measured as variable costs.

■ Can you identify anything you can do to improve the way you manage resources under your control?

_____

_____

_____

■ understand how standard costing techniques help to control cost.

Some organizations use standard costing which can be determined as ideal, expected or current standards. If used in your organization, do you feel that they are determined and used in the best way to motivate your workteam?

■ Make a note of improvements you could recommend or put into action.

_____

_____

_____

_____

Standard costs are used as a standard against which to measure our performance. Standard costing is a common way of arriving at variances from target, allowing first line managers to make adjustments and take action to keep costs down.

■ Do you feel that all standard costs identified in your work area are appropriate? Should you recommend to your manager that the standards should be altered, even if you found that standards were determined in a logical way? Why? Make a note of any changes you could propose.

_____

_____

_____

_____

■ Do you receive information about variances in a timely way? Would earlier receipt of information improve your effectiveness and how could this be achieved?

_____

_____

_____

_____

■ Use different methods for controlling and reducing costs.

To plan for the future, maintain control and measure performance we need detailed cost information. A good way of doing this is to allocate costs into cost centres against locations such as:

■ departments;
■ groups of machines;
■ individuals.

For cost centres to operate properly, first line managers need to record and communicate accurate information about the hours worked, idle time, material costs and so on.

■ Can you think of ways to improve communication in your workplace? Make a note of any suggestions you have for change below.

_____

_____

_____

■ Do you feel costs are appropriately allocated at present? Suggest changes for a fairer allocation below.

_____

_____

_____

Maintaining a good cost control system takes effort and can be frustrating, especially when you are working hard to keep the costs down but still finding it difficult to keep within budget. Controlling costs is a test of leadership. You will need to be aware of cost overruns, be able to communicate problems to management and your workteam, and involve your workteam in keeping costs down.

■ How do you communicate the importance of controlling costs? Do you use notices and change them regularly so they are not ignored? Do you talk directly to your workteam about cost control? Make a note of any improvements you feel you can make.

_____

_____

_____

_____

_____

■ Is cost control rewarded in your workplace? Should it be? Perhaps you have some thoughts you can write down now to discuss with your manager in the future.

_____

_____

_____

_____

■ Help to draw up workable budgets.

Budgets are a way of bringing together all an organization's plans and presenting them in a way that allows people to monitor their progress against them. As a first line manager you will be involved both in generating information for budget preparation and in ensuring that variances from budget are monitored and acted upon.

How are budgets prepared in your workplace? Is the sequence correct – is the budget that contains the limiting factor prepared first, and then communicated widely? Make notes of any areas in which you feel that the sequence or communication of budgeting is inadequate, and make suggestions for improvements.

_____

_____

_____

Are you involved in collecting information for the preparation of budgets? Is the information you collect actually used? What other items of information do you think would be useful? Are your budgets up to date? Make notes on any areas of your work where out-of-date budget information has presented you with difficulties.

_____

_____

_____

2 Action plan

Use this plan to further develop for yourself a course of action you want to take. Make a note in the left-hand column of the issues or problems you want to tackle, and then decide what you intend to do, and make a note in column 2.

The resources you need might include time, materials, information or money. You may need to negotiate for some of them, but they could be something easily acquired, like half an hour of somebody's time, or a chapter of a book. Put whatever you need in column 3. No plan means anything without a timescale, so put a realistic target completion date in column 4.

Finally, describe the outcome you want to achieve as a result of this plan, whether it is for your own benefit or advancement, or a more efficient way of doing things.

Desired outcomes					
1 Issues	2 Action		3 Resources	4 Target completion	
Actual outcomes					

3 Extensions

Extension 1   Book   *Simple and Practical Costing, Pricing and Credit Control*
            Author   Keith Kirkland and Stuart Howard
            Edition   First edition, 1998
            Publisher   Kogan Page

Extension 2   Book   *Financial Planning using Spreadsheets*
            Author   Sue Nugus
            Edition   First edition, 1997
            Publisher   Kogan Page

Extension 3   Book   *Cost Control: A Strategic Guide*
            Author   David Doyle
            Edition   First edition, 1994
            Publisher   Kogan Page

These extensions can be taken up via your ILM Centre. They will either have them or will arrange that you have access to them. However, it may be more convenient to check out the materials with your personnel or training people at work – they may well give you access. There are good reasons for approaching your own people; for example, they will become aware of your interest and you can involve them in your development.

4 Answers to self-assessment questions

Self-assessment 1 on page 17

1 Direct materials costs can be identified directly and in total with an item being produced, whereas indirect materials costs have a more general use in an organization and cannot be identified directly and in total.

2 As reporters have a regular wage and advertising staff receive commission:

- the wages of the advertising staff are VARIABLE COSTS;
- the wages of the reporters are FIXED COSTS.

3 a Direct labour cost CAN be TOTALLY identified with a particular product.
  b Wages which CANNOT be identified with a particular product are INDIRECT labour costs.
  c Direct labour costs are often VARIABLE costs because they increase or decrease in proportion to the production being carried out.

4 The break-even number of members is £18,000/£15 = 1,200 members.

5 The wastage of components used in the production of hard disks should be under Sam's control. Sam is not likely to be involved in marketing and sales so advertising is not controllable by Sam, nor is Sam's basic salary which would be set by senior managers.

Self-assessment 2 on pages 32–3

1 (a) A standard cost is a PREDETERMINED cost that is achieved by setting STANDARDS related to particular circumstances or conditions of work.

2 The two reasons for setting performance standards in any organization are:

- to base costs upon them;
- to measure actual performance.

3 The standard cost of a vase is £2.50, calculated as follows:

> **Standard cost sheet**
>
> Direct materials: £8.00 ÷ 4 = £2.00
> Direct wages: £7.50 ÷ 10 = £0.75
> £2.75

4   Direct material cost variances comprise a usage variance and a price variance. Direct labour cost variances comprise an efficiency variance, an idle time variance and a rate variance.

5   A favourable variance indicates that actual costs are less than standard costs. An adverse variance indicates that actual costs are greater than standard costs.

Self-assessment 3 on page 68

1   a   The components of prime cost are direct materials and direct labour.
    b   Factory overheads are added to prime cost to arrive at the total factory cost.

2   A cost centre is a location where costs can be identified, grouped together and then finally related to a cost unit.

3   A good cost system enables costs to be:

- collected:
- analysed;
- controlled.

4   The three keys to success are:

- Involvement;
- Communication;
- Feedback.

5   Workers should be provided with information in a form they can relate to and at a time and place where the cost is incurred.

6   A checklist helps to channel thoughts and avoids the possibility of overlooking matters.

Self-assessment 4 on page 85

1   The KEY or LIMITING factor is the factor on which all other budgets depend.

   This can be sales or production levels, cash or other aspects which mean that an organization cannot trade at a higher level without attention to the key factor itself.

2   The planned production level is calculated as follows.

   Sales 12,000 + 10% (1,200) = 13,200 units

   13,200 units less planned decrease in stock levels of 680
   (2,000 – 1,320) = 12,520 units

3   Details of birth rates and new-build local housing and (c) National pay awards are EXTERNAL sources of information. (b) Advice from teachers about the need for new books and equipment is INTERNAL.

4 Poor supervision of labour leads to poor timekeeping; of equipment use leads to breakdowns; and of materials usage can lead to pilferage.

5 Organizations maintain departmental budgets to define costs and responsibilities to specific cost centres.

5 Answers to Activities

**Activity 15
on pages 24–5**

Here are my completed calculations to compare with yours.

> **Standard cost sheet**
>
> | | |
> |---|---|
> | Direct materials: 5 metres at £6.10 | £30.50 |
> | Direct wages: | |
> | Moulder 1½ hours × £8.00 | £12.00 |
> | Cutter 2½ hours × £10.00 | £25.00 |
> | | £67.50 |

So the standard cost of a table is £67.50.

**Activity 24
on page 43**

Since some of our codes provide a group of numbers, your suggested cost codes may not be exactly the same as mine, but I hope you can see how cost codes are actually made up.

Here are the numbers I would use:

- Theatre 1 staff nurse's salary: 098 026
- Theatre 2 medical equipment: 099 400 (or any number to 449)
- Physiotherapy department medical equipment: 264 400
- Drug coded 459 and ordered for the pharmacy: 171 459
- Canteen cook's wages: 400 197

**Activity 28
on page 48**

I hope we can agree on the following figures:

Regular time 40 hours at £6.00	240.00
Overtime premium 3 hours at £9.00	27.00
Gross pay for week	£267.00

6 Answers to the quick quiz

**Quick quiz
on pages 87–8**

Answer 1   Sales − Costs = profit

Answer 2   Fixed costs are costs incurred whether anything is being produced or not.

Answer 3   As an indirect labour cost or overhead.

Answer 4   Some costs are incurred by the organization as a whole.

Answer 5   Ideal, expected or current standards.

Answer 6   To aid control and planning.

Answer 7   The workteam spent longer making the product than the standard indicated.

Answer 8   Costs and performance levels.

Answer 9   A location into which direct costs and overheads are gathered.

Answer 10   A cost code identifies particular types of cost and assists in analysis of the extent of these costs used in particular centres and throughout the organization.

Answer 11   Idle time is unproductive time – not spent on actual production.

Answer 12   Costs can only be controlled if the workteam is committed.

Answer 13   Through communication and feedback.

Answer 14   The limiting factor determines the level of activity at which the organization must plan to operate.

7 Certificate

Completion of this certificate by an authorized person shows that you have worked through all the parts of this workbook and satisfactorily completed the assessments. The certificate provides a record of what you have done that may be used for exemptions or as evidence of prior learning against other nationally certificated qualifications.

Pergamon Flexible Learning and ILM are always keen to refine and improve their products. One of the key sources of information to help this process are people who have just used the product. If you have any information or views, good or bad, please pass these on.

INSTITUTE OF LEADERSHIP & MANAGEMENT

SUPERSERIES

Controlling Costs

....

has satisfactorily completed this workbook

Name of signatory   ....

Position   ....

Signature   ....

Date   ....

Official stamp

Fourth Edition

INSTITUTE OF LEADERSHIP & MANAGEMENT
SUPERSERIES
FOURTH EDITION

To order – phone us direct for prices and availability details
(please quote ISBNs when ordering) on 01865 888190